A BEGINNER'S GUIDE TO NEARPOD

A Tool for Transforming
Virtual Teaching in K-12

"Olivia places the learning front and center. If you are looking for tips and strategies for student engagement and formative assessment, you'll want to check out this guide on using Nearpod!" - Monica Burns, Ed.D., author of Tasks Before Apps: Designing Rigorous Learning in a Tech-Rich Classroom

Olivia Odileke, M.Ed

Published by Kampus Insights Inc.

955 Croton Rd

Melbourne, FL 32935

Printed in the United States of America
Published 2021.

Library of Congress Control Number: 2020924898

ISBN 978-1-7363417-0-4

OliviaOdileke.com

First Paperback Edition

DEDICATION

This book is dedicated to all the first-year, virtual teachers who may have been forced to learn how to adapt to an ever changing EdTech infused education environment. We need you to adapt and press forward as you become learners of a new school of thought in elevating the achievement of all students and closing the achievement gaps of students from low socio-economic backgrounds. May this serve as a beginning to your lifelong journey of teaching with a high standard of excellence.

TABLE OF CONTENT

INTRODUCTION

———————— ♦◇♦ ————————

Thank you for taking time out of your busy education schedule to develop your skills as a virtual educator. I know you are probably wondering where you will find the time to read and then apply what you are learning. As you get a taste of what Nearpod can offer you and your students, you will become more curious about this tool. There are indeed many educational technology tools that are available to educators, but none compare to the features and constant innovation that Nearpod brings to education. I truly believe this tool has the needs of teachers at the heart of their operation and the company is committed to transforming education. As a National Certified Trainer for Nearpod, I have listened to thousands of teachers, who struggle with getting started using a new tool. I purposely wrote this book for my slow adaptors and for those who need to receive content in baby steps, in order to understand and apply the tool effectively.

I wanted to help more teachers gain the confidence to step out of their teaching norms and embrace a more elevated and accelerated means of reaching out to students, especially our special program populations and our lowest 25%. In order to bridge the gap, we must take our teaching methods to new heights and focus on what students are thinking. We need real time data that can help us inform our decisions just in time to meet the needs of our students. This can only be achieved one teacher at a time, taking education beyond a standardized test to the point that a student is able to think for themselves and reason on the evidence presented to them.

I know it can be scary unlearning hard-wired practices, but I believe you are on the path to greater things if you apply some of the principles presented in this book. Every day, I review videos of virtual classrooms, looking for tasks that have students thinking and being actively engaged in their learning. These occasions are rare because so many of us have been programmed to lecture and deliver content. In order to engage students, there needs to be a shift. Students must be actively participating in rigorous activities that keep them inquiring, researching, and exploring topics, to the point where their mind facilitates curiosity naturally. If you want students to be curious, you must provide learning experiences that require a little bit of ambiguity, where there is not always a right answer. If you feel that you are ready to journey into a place where a teacher sparks learning, then you have set yourself up for an excellent foundation to do so.

There are students who need you to breathe life into your content, and in turn, give them a life of possibilities. Teachers are the most powerful force in shaping the minds of a young person. I hope you build their character as well as their desire to learn one transformational lesson at a time. You are to be commended for investing in yourself. Just fifteen minutes of practicing a day in Nearpod can help you reshape the way you teach and build your confidence in tools you never knew existed. Welcome to the beginner's guide to transforming your virtual teaching.

PART I: MASTER THE FUNDAMENTALS

———— ♦◇♦ ————

An essential component of Nearpod's platform is its seamless flow into existing programs that educators have grown to love and accept as a part of their daily digital lessons. Virtual teachers may use Learning Management Systems such as Schoology, Canvas, Blackboard, or Google Classroom. Nearpod offers super easy integrations systems that make it user friendly to search for your Nearpod lessons right in those LMS platforms. Also, logging into the Nearpod platform is with just a Google or Microsoft email account, allowing educators to continue to use the programs that educators are already familiar with.

Unlike many educational tech tools that offer one primary focus, Nearpod is a powerful edtech platform that offers multiple options for achieving one goal. Since it is unique, there are a few fundamental tasks that need to be mastered in the beginning, that allow more complex functions to be added later in your usage of the tool. One basic function is deciding how you want to launch a lesson. Yes, Nearpod lessons are launched. They are not presented as in presentation software. Launch is a fitting word, as this tool is an interactive presentation tool and not just a tool for presenting. The Launch depends on how you want your students to interact with the content. Would you prefer they move through the lesson independently and work at a pace that is right for them with student-paced mode? Or would you prefer they work at your pace and have specified time for group interactions and discussions in synchronous mode? These two options shift the thinking of an educator, and create an avenue for students to have a choice and to meet students where they are.

Another basic function is knowing how each feature functions within a lesson, what features collect data and which features do not. The goal is not to just insert any type of feature because we assume all the features are interactive. The true goal is to be intentional about how you want students to interact with content in relation to your underlying learning goal, then determine how you want the student to practice and show mastery of the learning goal. If this is how you approach this tool, it will produce your desired outcomes and you will find more joy in your art of teaching.

The last basic function to master is how to create your content or import content from other presentation tools into Nearpod. The tool is designed to make it easy to take existing Google Slides, Microsoft PowerPoints, or PDF presentations and import them into the program or use an add-on to insert interactive features. The type of presentation you want to transform into a Nearpod lesson will dictate the method used for that purpose.

This book is dedicated to mastering these fundamental functions and increasing your comfort in practicing the basics of Nearpod. There are also video tutorials which are linked in the resources section of the book that accompany these chapters, to help you read it, see it, and provide you the opportunity to do it. The ideal goal is to practice using the tool at least 15 minutes a day. The beginning is always the hardest, but without a struggle there can be no progress. If you do this one simple task, you will feel rejuvenated and your curiosity will help you to keep mastering the fundamentals of this powerful tool.

CHAPTER ONE: HOW NEARPOD BENEFITS VIRTUAL TEACHERS

There's a way to do it better-find it. -**Thomas Edison**

Imagine having a class size of 200 virtual students and your primary means of communication is only email, with only one monthly check in call with each student. You meet your students 2-3 times a week for a live class session, but only about 70% of the students show up to your virtual classes consistently. Your content area has standardized tests at the end of each school year. It requires you to teach and access the learning levels of your students regularly. They expect you to prepare students for the rigor of a standardized test. **How can you achieve this goal when you are faced with these limitations? How can you ensure all students have access to the content and that rigor is built into your lessons, even when students are absent from a live session? How can you create engaging content with rich lessons, that meet the needs of all your learners? Or how can you tie in an existing online curriculum to help students go deeper into their content topics?** These are real situations for virtual teachers and even more so, for teachers who may have been forced to convert their teaching to strictly virtual overnight.

The scenario just described was me as a new virtual teacher. One thing about virtual lessons is that they require more time and energy to plan than a traditional lesson. You have to be purposeful in each slide, instructions must be explicit, small group discussions must be orchestrated to ensure student participation, questions must be selected that give rise to lively conversations, technology issues must be considered. **What procedure will you put into place for virtual behavior?** You must plan intentional interaction with content or students, which may drift onto other online activities, and plan for how data will be collected is crucial in the instructional process. Additionally, when planning for technology use, you must consider how students will log into the tool. Consider if provision for usernames and passwords need to be made. **Will there be connectivity issues? How will you share your lesson with students who are absent, and how will you make them more accountable for participation with your live sessions and returning assignments?**

Many of us are familiar with classroom procedures and expectations, but how does that translate to virtual learning? Can we expect the same as we would, if we were in the classroom? Virtual teaching requires a paradigm shift in our thinking and how we approach learning overall. This shift requires a teacher to think outside of the box and develop activities that can be completed independently, with the purpose of academically engaging the student. We cannot fall into the habit of planning activities for only engagement purposes or to just have students doing something. We must require students to demonstrate their understanding and explain their thinking, even when a teacher is not physically there. So, how can a virtual teacher do this and make students more accountable?

One easy way to make a student accountable is setting the expectation that every item submitted is checked by a teacher and feedback is provided to the student and even the parents or guardians. This decreases the chances of a student not completing a lesson or participating in a live session because the student knows you are aware of the work they have done or are presently completing.

How can a teacher do this?

Most teachers use Google docs or a pre-existing online curriculum to deliver assessments, which determine how a student performed in a lesson. But, if a teacher is not physically with a student or cannot see a student, the discord is how they provide formative assessments to gather the information they need to adjust their instruction. These are a few dilemmas of a virtual teacher and there are limited one stop online technology tools that can respond to these needs effectively. Virtual teachers need online tech tools that are easy access for both teacher and student; that provide the data they need when they need it, offer features that allow students to interact with the content in multiple ways, provide instant feedback so students can overcome misconceptions—and tools that make it easy for students to be creative and openly explain their thinking to their peers and their teachers. As a virtual teacher, Nearpod gave me a power tool that would enable me to increase my efficiency as a teacher and decrease the amount of time I spent planning instruction and grading assignments. Let's discuss some of the key benefits that Nearpod offers to the virtual teacher.

BENEFIT 1: REAL-TIME DATA

No more waiting until the end of the day to review exit tickets, to see who got the lesson or who needs to be retaught a lesson. One benefit of this tool is that many of the student activity features allow you to review their responses in real time. For example, students can complete a worksheet in the Draw It feature and while the student is typing, the teacher is able to see their responses in progress. Once the student submits their responses, you can review it and if needed, ask the student to resubmit or give the student a hint that will allow them to complete the worksheet. You can also pose an Open-Ended Question, which enables you to see each student's responses and even share the responses that meet the expectations of the posed question with the entire class. You can provide a check for understanding assessment and after each one is submitted, you can see what questions were answered correctly and incorrectly. If you notice a pattern on one question you can plan another lesson to help students overcome their misunderstanding. This is one the most powerful reasons that technology tools are used in a classroom—to overcome misconceptions and increase the depths of understanding. Provide the immediate feedback that students need in a non-stressful environment, to help students learn from their mistakes and even provide discussion opportunities. Students would then describe what strategies they used to arrive at their explanations. Research shows that if feedback is not provided in 24 hours, then it is ineffective in combating a student's misconception. By providing more natural stops for informing your instruction and giving students what they need in the moment, you elevate your instructional delivery and increase the content retention of the student.

BENEFIT 2: INTERACTIVE FEATURES

As humans, we thrive on interaction. One reason social media is so popular among students is that it is interactive. You have a public audience that you can post comments, photos, or videos and receive direct communication from persons who like, dislike, agree, or disagree with your posts. Many students spend a large portion of their day on social media sites, because they thrive on interactions with others. 21st century lessons must also be designed to provide opportunities for interaction. The days of standing in front of the class and providing a twenty plus minutes lecture, and then providing time to read and answer questions are gone. The content must be relevant and provide natural breaks that command interaction and full student engagement. The interactive features in Nearpod focus on providing activities that require the student demonstrate or do something to show what they know or what they do not know about the content. These interactive features include: Poll, Open Ended Questions (with the option for written or audio response!), a Quiz, a Draw It, a gamified quiz calledTime to Climb, Matching Pairs, Collaborate Board, Fill in the Blanks, and a memory test. Each interactive activity gathers data from a student. You can review this data from the Reports tab of your Nearpod Account, and see data in-the-moment while teaching. You no longer need to have students answer questions from a book, but you have the power to include a variety of activities into your lesson, that provide both you and the student feedback and further command their attention towards content being presented. These activities even allow you to add reference material to a question, so students can refer back to content or dig deeper into content already presented. You can add an image, an audio file, a website, a video, or a pdf to most activities. This allows students with accommodations to have equal access to the activities by providing built in supports. We will discuss each feature in more detail, alongside ideas of how best to use it in a lesson.

BENEFIT 3: EASY ACCESS TO LESSONS

The application works on ANY mobile device—including tablets, iPads, and smartphones. This causes less technical issues arising from students or parents trying to access the lessons. Unlike most apps that require a student login name and password, Nearpod just provides your students with a code or a direct link to the lesson. Students enter the code to access the lesson and type their first and last name to join your lesson. There is an optional student name validation feature in the advanced settings of your account. This will require the student to login into their Single Sign On account and auto fill their name. This is a good practice if you have young students' login in, as they may just type their first name and if they are multiple students with that name, there may be confusion. Students do not need Nearpod accounts to access your lesson. They just need a code and you need a system to ensure they enter their correct name, so that you can provide the student with credit and view their activities in Reports.

Another benefit is that you never need to worry about having your lessons saved to your computer or a jump drive. All of your lessons are stored in your online Nearpod account and can be accessed from any device with internet connection. You can easily make quick adjustments to any lesson by clicking on the edit button. This is also an added benefit in case you leave your PC somewhere or you run into a technical problem with one of your devices. I highly recommend creating lesson folders to keep your lesson content organized and limit the amount of time you spend trying to find a lesson you have created in the past.

BENEFIT 4: MULTIPLE WAYS TO REACH LEARNERS

One of the most powerful benefits of using Nearpod is that you can reach all learners by adjusting the way you deliver content. As you design your lessons, you want to present your content in three ways. You present in three ways to reach your three types of learners. There are three main cognitive learning styles: Visual, Auditory, and Kinesthetic. Visual learners need pictures, charts, graphs, and opportunities to see the information in action. Auditory learners tend to retain information more through hearing and speaking. The Kinesthetic learners like the hands-on approach to learning and prefer to demonstrate their learning as against verbalizing it. As a traditional teacher, it is a challenge to provide engaging, interactive content that is purposefully designed to meet all three cognitive learning styles. However, as a virtual teacher you have more options to meet the needs of all your learners, by providing multiple ways for students to access content with little time exerted to do so. In the section on lesson plan design, I go deeper into how to incorporate each learning style into your very own lessons.

KEY POINT

Nearpod was designed to give teachers a tool for increasing the engagement of students. This is most needed for virtual students, as there are many barriers to engaging with an audience that you may never see visually. With a virtual tool that provides you with real time data, provides a variety of interactive features, can be easily accessed by anyone, and can be used to meet the learning styles of multiple learners, there are simply more possibilities than with traditional presentation tools.

In the next chapter, you will learn how to focus on the most important thing and how this never changes.

CHAPTER TWO: FOCUS ON THE MOST IMPORTANT THING

We are what we repeatedly do, excellence then is not an act, but a habit. **–Aristotle**

The main purpose of a teacher is to teach. No educational technology tool can teach a student. It can only support or supplement what effective teaching practices you already have. There is no magic app that can get students to achieve high academic success. Study after study shows that the teacher has the greatest effect on the academic outcomes of students, no matter their ethnicity, race, or socio-economic backgrounds. I beg you not to abandon your sound instructional pedagogy. You would rather find ways to enhance your instructional practices, by exploring more creative ways for students to demonstrate mastery and have access to your content area. Also, the purpose is to find ways to make more efficient use of your time and energy.

Let's illustrate it this way! Imagine yourself as an excellent cook. You have been making delicious meals from scratch for more than a decade. Your meals usually take you about 1 to 2 hours to prepare and you spend most of your time preparing the ingredients for your meals. You only have two knives and you only use the stove or the oven to cook your meals. On the other hand, imagine you are still an excellent cook who makes meals from scratch, but has additional tools to help prepare your meals. You have an air fryer to manage your fried foods and make them healthier. You have a power pressure cooker that allows you to cook frozen food in a fraction of the time. You have a process that allows you to cut up vegetables faster with less waste. You can cook food items with your induction cooker, by setting a timer that will turn off your food while you take a quick shower before dinner. With these tools, you can have a full meal ready in less than 45 minutes. Of the two types of cookers, which one are you? Both are still excellent cooks, but one does it more efficiently and uses less time. As a teacher, we still do our most important work of teaching students to mastery their content standards. The methods we use can help increase our productivity, better inform our daily instructional decisions, and help us focus on the most important thing which is teaching.

Hence, we don't stop teaching, but rather, enhance our teaching with tools that make us more efficient and allow us buy back some of our personal time. As we focus on the most important thing, let's shift our focus to the learning goal. Every effective teacher starts with an intentional learning goal for the lesson, based on the underlying academic standard driving that goal. Let's focus on how starting with the learning goal can empower you to utilize Nearpod features.

THE LEARNING GOAL

The learning goal is important because they:

1. Provide students with a clear purpose to focus their learning.
2. Provide insights on what instructional activities to choose and guide your selection of types of assessments to use.

There are many books written on how to develop learning goals and how to turn a learning goal into specific learning objectives. You can check out those books, which help in crafting a learning goal. There are two components of a learning goal that I tend to focus on: (1) What I want my students to know and (2) What I want my students to do with the obtained knowledge. As a teacher, I focus on two things: Contents I need to help students learn this concept and what activities my students can do to ensure they have mastered the content. These are the most important things I consider in planning an effective lesson. It is not enough to have a student recall information, but it is the application of the knowledge gain, that will drive higher student achievement and retention of content presented. When teachers do this, they do not get distracted by many educational technology features being presented to them. Instead, they can shift through the ample amount of resources to carefully select the feature that will allow them to accomplish their target learning goal.

This phase of lesson planning provides you the most creativity and helps you imagine how your students will learn and interact with your lesson to achieve their own personal results. As a teacher, I imagine myself as my students and think about how they will feel as they interact with the content presented. I try to have empathy for them and think about ways I can make the lessons simple, but keep it intellectually engaging, so as to make them critical thinkers. One of the main goals of my teaching is to stimulate thinking. My purpose is to make their heads hurt a little so as to help them reach their thinking potential. It is not about preparing a student for a standardized test, but it is preparing my students for the life tests that only critical thinkers can pass. That, to me, is the most important thing. If this is your focus and your passion too, you will excel as a virtual teacher. We want students to THINK and not regurgitate information. The online environment creates a perfect opportunity for students to connect with real world audiences and discuss topics that go beyond the classroom. You will find yourself on a path that enables students to truly become lifelong learners.

As a teacher, I never stop learning! I stay curious about things and try to find new ways to use old tools. There is so much to learn with so much information available on the internet. My hope is that you never stop learning either.

You are already in a class by yourself because you have taken the time to invest in yourself, by exploring a new tool to support the most important thing that you do.

USE THE LEARNING GOAL TO BUILD INTERACTIVE LESSONS

Since we know that the learning goal is the most important thing, how can we transfer those important things to a Nearpod lesson? I am confident that you know how to create a learning goal and you probably have a firm hold on creating or locating assessments that can help you measure student mastery. However, the most important reason for reading this book is to learn how I used Nearpod's features to build interactive lessons. So, let's start with a sample learning goal and I will show you how to build content to help us focus on what we want students to know. Afterwards, we find and create activities that focus on what students can do. Let's look at an example from a sixth-grade math standard in geometry. This is a two-part standard, but we will focus on the second part of the standard.

Common Core Standard: MGSE6.G.2 Apply formulas V= (length) X (width) x (height) and V=(area of base) x (height) to find volumes of right rectangular prisms with fractional edge lengths in the context of solving real world and mathematical problems.

Learning Goal: Students will be able to compare two-dimensional rectangles and a three-dimensional rectangular prism and label each side of the prism. With this knowledge, students will make connections between finding the area of a two-dimensional shape and apply the Volume formula to a variety of real-world word problems involving rectangular prisms, both teacher made and student generated.

What do I want my students to know?

I want my students to know the difference between a 2D object and a 3D object. I want my students to know the difference between area and volume. I want my student to know the area formula for a rectangle and the volume formula for a rectangular prism. I want them to know the difference between a rectangle and a rectangular prism.

What do I want my student to do?

I want my students to read word problems, identifying the height, length, and width of the shape in the word problem. I want students to write out the volume formula and substitute the corresponding side with the correct label. I want students to generate their own volume word problems and have other students solve it.

By starting with a clear picture of what I want my students to know and to do, I can start to select activities that will reinforce the most important thing in my lesson(s).

This learning goal will require at least three lessons to accomplish the learning goal. After determining that goal, I incorporate the features in Nearpod to help me more efficiently accomplish my learning goal. Starting with the learning goal in mind will set you up for success using any virtual platform to deliver your lessons, and this skill can be harnessed no matter what your technology skill level is. Successful planning with technology relies on your ability to unpack the standard and focus on what students will know and do. Here is another example using a fourth-grade science standard in Earth Science:

Florida State Standard: SC.4. E.6.1 Identify the three categories of rocks: Igneous, (formed from molten rock); sedimentary (pieces of other rocks and fossilized organisms); and metamorphic (formed from heat and pressure).

Learning Goal: Students will explore the three categories of rocks and what makes each type of rock unique. Students will be given different types of rocks and asked to describe the characteristics of each rock.

What do I want my students to know?

I want my students to know the three categories of rocks, by reviewing a definition and by examining an image or video of the rock.

What do I want my student to do?

I want my students to describe each category of rock by writing a written description to go with preselected images of three types of rocks.

The learning goal is focused on knowing the three types of rocks and then being able to write in their own words, a description based on looking at an image of a rock. This description would also identify the type of rock the image represents and included descriptors that point to that fact. This process becomes easier the more you do it and this one step will help make your lessons more engaging and meaningful to your students.

Overall, your learning goal will help you select the best content and activities, which are Nearpod features, to add to your Nearpod Lesson. The content features will be directly linked to what you want students to know and the activity features will be directly linked to what you want your students to do. By dividing the learning goal into two parts, you can easily add content and activities that reinforce your learning goal and optimize your student's learning efforts with ease.

KEY POINT

The most important thing is teaching with a well-defined learning goal. This learning goal is broken into two components: what you want students to know and what you want students to do. Once this is clearly established, you will then place content items under what you want students to know and activity items under what you want students to do. In Nearpod, you have two types of features to add to your lesson: Content or Activities.

Content   Activities

Figure 2-1 Add Slide contains these two categories

When you start with the end in mind, it will make it easier to choose the best activities or content types to add to your lesson. In the next chapter, you will learn the basics navigation of Nearpod and how to set your preferences in your account settings.

CHAPTER THREE: THE BASICS

The most positive way to progress to the top is to start at the bottom and never stop. – **Anonymous**

This chapter will cover the base or essential part of Nearpod. Nearpod is simply an interactive presentation tool that serves as an effective tool to increase student engagement. Most of us are familiar with presentations tools such as PowerPoint, Keynote, and Google Slides. These presentation tools allow you to add text, images, and video to your presentations and infuse color and creativity in your slide design. But we know that students need more than information presented to them. These new generations of students crave interaction and instant feedback. Nearpod adds the interactive features students crave and infused media-rich content, to help increase student's engagement with academic content. In other words, it meets the needs of students by allowing access to lessons on ANY device and with the type of interactive features that make a student want to fully participate. All teachers want 100% participation from students, and some of us have achieved it in our own rights. However, with so many apps and online sites competing for our student's attention, we need modern tools to help solve our participation problem, especially when you have virtual students. To sum it up, Nearpod is an interactive instructional tool that increases student engagement for virtual students and allows you easy access to full session reports that can be used to consistently direct your instruction daily.

Now that we know what Nearpod is—an interactive instructional tool—what's next? Creating a free Nearpod Silver account is a great place to get started. However, the Gold account option unlocks more storage space to create and download more lessons (1GB compared to 100MB in the free version), and enhanced features like more students per lesson and Nearpod Sub Plans., so I highly recommend getting a paid account or at least trying it out. In the resources tab, I provide a code that is good for a 3-month upgrade to a Gold Account. Once you taste Gold, it will be very hard to ever go back to Silver. If you are going to use Nearpod, it makes sense to have access to all of the features and never think twice about what you might be missing. You can easily login using your Gmail or your Office 365 credentials at nearpod.com. Once you login, you will always land in your personal Nearpod Library, which will look empty until you start to add your own lessons or ready-made lessons from the Nearpod library. Let's go over what's included in the navigation bar.

NEARPOD NAVIGATION

The navigation bar is located on the left side and has four main categories. Let's review each category.

My Materials: **My Lessons** is where your own lessons or lessons you have added from the Nearpod Library will be stored. **Reports** is where you will find the data from activities embedded within your lessons. **Sub Plans** is an excellent feature, available with any paid license, as it allows you to share your Nearpod lesson sub plans with a substitute or administrator and have this lesson ready to be used by your substitute. No more boring lessons for your substitute. If they have a smart device, they can launch the lesson right from their phones. Yes or Yes!

Shared Libraries: If your school or district purchases a license, these libraries allow a school to share lessons with the entire staff. There is a **School Library** and a **District Library**. This is also great for team teaching or sharing resources within a grade level. Any teacher can add lessons to the School Library, and District Admin can curate content in the District Library. Lessons can also be mapped out per nine weeks, so that teams can access content and have more meaningful discussion around the data trends they collect from their Reports. This one feature can help facilitate more objective conversations about what students know and where we want to take students in their learning journey. It also creates more synergistic opportunities to transform the learning for both the students and the teachers. It makes instructional data meetings more transparent and helps strengthen even the weakest teachers at the school.

Nearpod Content: The primary place to get access to over 7,500 ready-made lessons and over 2,000 videos and activities is the **Nearpod Library**. This library includes full lessons, warmups, skill builders, virtual reality tours, and includes interactive videos with discussion questions built in. Plus, you can search by your standards to quickly find resources for your plans. Nearpod also offers Premium Collections for schools and districts who want to customize their Nearpod package with specific content aligned to their initiatives or strategic plan. These other libraries include:

- Nearpod Learning Labs - A Ready Made Interactive Professional Development training that can be easily adjusted to meet the PD goals of any school.
- English Learners - Lessons dedicated to helping English Learners gain access to academic content faster and more intentionally.
- Digital Citizenship & Literacy - A library of lessons designed to empower students to use technology responsibly, safely, and effectively.
- College & Career Exploration - A library of lessons focused on developing the whole-child and providing exposure to college campuses and career related skills

- Historical Perspectives & Literacy - A library of lessons focused on bringing more perspective to history, with a modern twist on events.
- Social & Emotional Learning - A library of lessons dedicated to meeting the social and emotional needs of students beyond the classroom.
- Flocabulary Video Pack - A library of hip hop vocabulary lessons that bring academic content to a new world of animation and creative expression.

Resources: Under this tab is where you find Teacher Resources. **Teacher Resources** is directly linked to on-demand webinars, self-paced lessons on features related to Nearpod, and related tips in using Nearpod effectively in the classroom.

At the top of the navigation bar, you can join a lesson provided by code. This is great for staff meetings, when a staff member wants to present information from their Nearpod account. All they need to do is provide that code and everyone can easily join the presentation. No projector is needed; everyone can view the presentation from their own personal devices.

LESSON SETTINGS

One place with your Nearpod account you want to become very familiar with is your Lesson settings. This tab located under your photo or silhouette on the top right, will allow you to control features within your Nearpod Lessons. Let's review each feature and when you may want to use this feature.

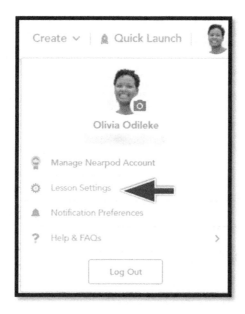

Figure 3 Lesson Settings Feature

These features are located under the *Lesson Settings* then click on *Advanced* tab in the left navigation bar. Here is a detail overview of each feature:

Enable student names to autofill- Students can be required to login using their Google or 365 account, but this works only on a PC or in the iOS app. This ensures that students first and last names are automatically filled when joining the session.

Enable Immersive Reader- This will allow texts to be read to students and can translate the text to any of the 100 languages available. This feature works with text created within Nearpod on a slide or text from a Google Slides presentation, as well as in most activities.

Enable Student Notes- This allows students to take notes and have the notes emailed to them or saved to their OneDrive or Google Drive.

Show quiz and multiple-choice questions results in Student-Paced mode- If you want students to have instant access to how they performed on a quiz, then you may want to turn on this feature. You may decide to turn it off when you use Nearpod as a graded assessment.

Allow students to resubmit answers in Live Participation mode- This feature is great when students do not submit answers that correspond to the question asked. This also works great when you have further clarity to a question and students want to redo their submitted response.

Enable Collaborate Board for Student-Paced lessons- When a student is in Student-Paced mode and a Collaborate Board is presented, their responses will stay there even when other students join the self-paced lesson. This is a great way for virtual learners to feel connected by reviewing the thoughts and comments of their peers, even asynchronously, but you should turn off the feature if you have concerns about students posting to a shared board while you're not online to monitor. As a teacher, you are able to delete comments from the reports tab, or by using the Teacher View, which is now available for Student-Paced mode.

Require student submissions- This feature works in the self-paced mode and will not allow a student to move to the next content slide or activity without submitting a response to the activity given.

Each of these features give you flexibility as a teacher to make features available when you need them. These will serve to ensure that students are meeting your expectations and allow you to set them for each of your Nearpod lessons when the time is needed.

KEY POINT

You should feel confident about the tabs available on the Navigation toolbar and how to turn on or off advanced features within your lesson settings. Some key tabs that you will use more frequently include the **My Library** tab and the **Nearpod Library** tab. All of the lessons you find in the Nearpod library will eventually be added to your library, for easy access to editing the lesson or launching the lesson with your students.

In the next chapter, we will discover how Nearpod is used to transform virtual learning and dive deeper into how we create and search for lessons.

PART II: PRACTICE MAKES PERMANENT

———— ♦◇♦ ————

The most fundamental way to build your skill in the use of any EdTech tool is to make time to practice using the tool. It seems like a simple concept, but way too often, I hear teachers say they just don't have the time to learn how to do something new. They feel confident about the tools that they are already using. My question to this is, are you getting the results from your standardized tests that prove your methods are producing the highest academic gains? Are all your students able to access the content and are you able to consistently collect data on the work produced by each of your students? How do you provide students with choice in your lessons? How do you regularly provide feedback so that students get what they need to combat misconceptions? If you find those questions hard to answer, then you may want to make some time to learn new tools that will help you reach more of your learners. If you know a teacher that this applies to, you may want to share this book with them.

It's not easy to find time to learn, but as curious learners, we must make the time to be more for our students—for the critical challenges that are facing education and the way students learn. I consider myself a research-based practitioner, who is always looking for research to be done. What research is available on *what an effective mathematics classroom looks like*? What is the teacher doing? What is the student doing? What does research say an effective Language Arts classroom looks like? What types of questions and activities are being discussed in that classroom?

These types of questions will drive a learner to seek tools, resources, and classroom practices that promote this type of thinking. What you may discover, may help you foster more resilience and confidence in your instructional practices and help improve your delivery.

When we focus on what we can control, our circle of influence increases. We find ourselves less annoyed by practices or policies that don't support teachers or students, and we put more energy on what matters the most. Inspiring a child to do something productive with their lives is the greatest source of happiness a person can have. I hope that the work I do each day inspires a teacher or a student to want to do more and be more, not because of how much money they will make, but by how many people they can influence to do what is right, to help those who are need, and to give when it is in your power to do so. Teaching helps me focus on others and not on myself. It helps me give without expecting anything in return. It helps me serve my purpose as a human and continue to enjoy my human experience, by going beyond the boundaries of the virtual classroom. Life is for living and I want to encourage you to live more, by acquiring skills that will help you reach and help more learners than you initially deemed possible.

We practice so that the skills we learn will become permanent. There is no such thing as perfection, but the more you practice the skills in the next few chapters, the more you will build your confidence and feel ready to tackle any learning goal that demands you implement interactive features to meet the needs of all your learners. Max on and max off, my fellow teacher, until you master the fundamentals of virtual teaching.

CHAPTER FOUR: USING NEARPOD TO TRANSFORM VIRTUAL LEARNING

Imagination is more important than knowledge -
Albert Einstein

Virtual learning seems like a simple undertaking. If you have a computer and have a teacher, it will be easy to create lessons for students to easily access online. However, a review of the virtual learning timeline will show that virtual learning has been a very boring affair. Many state mandated virtual programs consist of sound instructional design practices, where you begin with the end in mind. The objectives are specific, and the learning outcomes are measurable. Students are generally able to login into a Learning Management System where they can easily access the academic content, review course materials, participate in discussions, submit assignments, and complete assessments at their own pace and receive teacher feedback through written comments or scored assessments. This type of model is one of the primary reasons' parents choose virtual—because of the freedom to individualize the pace of when the course is completed.

However, this model typically has teachers in the background spending most of their time grading and providing individual feedback on assignments. Teachers may also offer live tutoring or online help sessions to help students progress through the curriculum. Students will spend most of their time reading and complete exercises with the online lesson. Some other virtual learning models have an online curriculum but supplement that curriculum by offering teacher-led virtual lessons, where a PowerPoint or Google Slides is traditionally used to present the lesson. This model may also limit student responses to chat, polls, using the microphone, or providing google docs or forms links for students to respond to questions in class. Also, the ideal of interactive lessons is usually limited to website links that students explore for an academic subject but often not built into the actual lesson themselves. This model provides the student with a sense of traditional learning, gives them an opportunity to interact socially with their peers and engage in whole group discussions about a topic.

Another limitation of more traditional virtual learning models, is the system's ability to offer more frequent formative assessments and capture real time data of the assessment that informs the teacher of the student's needs and then provide specific feedback and/ or a choice in differentiating the content, to help the student better comprehend the content. This is a real challenge. In the classroom, a teacher could at least see when a student is facing a challenge in learning, but how does the virtual teacher know the specific challenges of each student, when most students will just be a name with a voice but no face?

COVID-19 VIRTUAL LEARNING

Another virtual learning model was added during Covid-19. This model had teachers being the primary source of content. Most school districts did not have a universal online curriculum through which all students could login and complete self-paced lessons on their own. Instead, many districts employed Zoom, Google Meets, and WebEx to host their virtual classrooms. Many posted assignments to a Learning Management System like Google Classrooms, Canvas, Blackboard, or Schoology, and had students submit assignments electronically while providing written feedback. Some districts required live classes every day, while others allowed teachers to plan one to two live lessons or live help sessions. Some districts had teachers just email assignments weekly for their grading, with just weekly check in on how students were doing.

Since every district had different perspectives on how to deliver virtual learning to students, a lot of teachers were overwhelmed as no one had a clear understanding of what they were doing and what their primary purpose was. Was it to help students receive standard instruction or was it to give them some work to do while they were physically out of school? Additionally, teachers had their children at home and were faced with educating their own children while providing instructions for their classrooms online. In all of the confusion, teachers became afraid because what they once knew had become uncertain.

One of the biggest issues with virtual learning on this scale is the uncertainty. Teachers are scrambled with how to collect consistent data that can be used to inform my instruction, how to provide virtual interventions to help students who struggle, how to keep students academically engaged when we are not in a physical classroom, how to get feedback on my instructions, since this does not fit into my districts evaluation tool and how to use my limited time wisely to accomplish these things and provide feedback to my students. These are the types of questions teachers need answers too. Once these answers are laid out in a simple-to-follow way, the uncertainty diminishes, and teachers begin to have more confidence about what they do best—TEACH.

With all these virtual learning models, one common denominator is present. Students receive lessons by video or text using an LMS or presentation tool and are required to complete an assignment or assessment to earn credit. Some models provide live teacher sessions whereas some models do not. Overall, students are primarily required to read through academic content to answer questions, write essays, or complete assessments. These virtual learning models need to be renovated and rejuvenated. Let's focus on how Nearpod is and will continue to transform virtual learning.

TRANSFORMING VIRTUAL LEARNING

If more teachers had access to ready-made, standard-based, and interactive-focused lessons there would be less stress over the transition to virtual learning. But, one huge time taker for virtual teachers who teach live classes, is planning well designed online lessons. An online lesson takes twice the time to plan than a traditional lesson. It is due to the purposeful and very detailed planning that most go into well executed lessons. These lessons can never be impromptu and happen by chance. One way Nearpod transforms virtual learning is by giving teachers access to over 8,500 standard-aligned lessons in core and supplemental content academic subjects.

The real gem is that these lessons are designed to transform learning by engaging students in tasks that spark their curiosity and provide natural mediums to have in-depth discussions about the topics that they are learning. They are also excellent examples of what you as a teacher can create by yourself in Nearpod. The more exposure virtual teachers have to rich content and highly interactive lessons the more the desire to adjust current teaching practices and adapt to practices that help students learn and think about topics more deeply.

Transforming a lesson is also related to how a student can access that lesson. If a student can only access a lesson using one method only, you have limited that student to equal access. Equity in learning is increased when students do not have a barrier in how they access a lesson. Nearpod allows students to connect to lessons on any device that has Wi-Fi. This means that students are not limited to having only a computer or laptop. This opens the door to students who have limited access to technology and Wi-Fi connections. This means everyone can learn.

Content can also be presented in a synchronous environment or an asynchronous environment. This implies that teachers have more options in delivering their lessons. It also allows students who miss online lessons to have the lesson provided to them in a Student-Paced mode. This means, no student has to miss a lesson due to technical issues or being absent. This also provides virtual teachers with the power to teach whole group classes, do checks for understanding, and provide differentiation via Student-Paced lessons—right in the middle of a live class.

As stated before, transforming virtual learning means giving teachers options on how and when a lesson can be accessed. These options are coupled with real time data collection systems that allow you to review reports of each activity a student completes, whether in a live or self-paced session

Lessons must offer real world connections. By offering Virtual Reality (VR) Field Trips, teachers are able to transform a lesson by taking their students to places they would never be able to fundraise for. You take your students to a setting from a story, a historical location in social studies, to the residence of a scientist or mathematician, providing context to an academic topic, and so much more. It is only so limited in your imagination, what you can inspire in your students by just taking them on a VR Field Trip. Education should inspire us to be more curious and to want to explore content topics more, even if not for a grade. This is the underlying purpose of transforming virtual learning. To boldly take our students to places that they have never gone. To do that, we must create tech infused lessons that go beyond presenting content, by providing ample opportunities for students to interact with the content and with their peers, in rigorous tasks that promote thinking, exploring, and researching.

Lessons must offer appropriate tools where students can manipulate tools to determine patterns, trends, cause and effects, and make more meaningful connections to natural relationships explained in textbooks. Students need conceptual references as they make connections to apply the procedural components of standards. By offering stimulations, graphing calculators, and even 3-D models, Nearpod helps students to build concrete examples that help form long term connections to their long-term memory. When these connections are made, students retain concepts much longer than written text. Interaction promotes long term memory verses students reading text only to take an assessment to pass a test. A Nearpod lesson is more than helping a student pass a test, it is focused on equipping students to be learners and to tinker with their learning to enable them to stay curious. A curious student will always go beyond what you teach and that, my teacher friend, is the essence of why Nearpod is and will continue to transform virtual learning and traditional education.

KEY POINT

Traditional virtual learning has not fully explored ways to offer more interactive and academic engaging content that can reach all learners and provide teachers with real time data that can be used to drive their instruction. Virtual learning must go beyond playing videos, reading virtual textbooks, and completing assignments or assessments for credit. In order to transform virtual learning, all students need access to lessons. Content must make real world connections, appropriate tools need to be made available to help students connect concepts to procedures, and teachers need access to ready-made lessons to more easily differentiated lessons and decrease planning time for virtual lessons. Nearpod integrates with the video conferencing software and offers virtual teachers an accessible way to meet students in live settings, providing engaging and discussion-rich virtual lessons.

In the next chapter, we will explore what ready-made lessons are and how to search and edit these lessons for your next virtual class.

CHAPTER FIVE: GETTING STARTED WITH READY MADE LESSONS

Whether you think you can or think you can't, you are right. -**Henry Ford**

Have you ever wanted to video the lesson plans of effective teachers at your school or to review their PowerPoint decks for more creative ways to introduce topics to your students? Any reflective teacher desires to know what works for academically engaging students. You are now welcomed to the world of effective instruction through Nearpod's ready-made lesson library. So, what are ready-made lessons? Nearpod has partnered with over 60 educational publishing companies to offer teachers research-based instructional modeled lessons that can be customized to meet the unique needs of your students. Instead of spending hours trying to develop engaging and standard-based lessons, many can be previewed quickly and adjusted in less than 30 minutes to meet your needs. With Nearpod, you have access to over 7,000 lessons and thousands of videos and activities that are visually appealing and offer intentional questioning that builds on Bloom's Taxonomy without you overthinking it. You can download as many of these lessons as you'd like, up to your storage limit. Other benefits of using ready-made lessons is that you receive more exposure to lessons that have been structured to dive deeper into the academic content. Many of these lessons incorporate real world connections by adding VR Field Trips to help drive deeper understandings of content topics. Furthermore, lessons also incorporate metacognitive reflection opportunities, so that students reflect on their learning. In addition to the ready-made slide-based lessons housed in the Nearpod Library, there are also over 1,000 interactive videos with embedded questions ready for teachers to use quickly and easily.

The advantage of ready-made lessons and videos is that you get to spend more of your time making instructional decisions and designing effective interventions, while Nearpod helps empower virtual teachers to quickly get started in delivering digital instruction. This helps a teacher focus on the most important thing which is teaching. So now that we have discussed the value of ready-made lessons and videos, let's discuss how to search for lessons in the Nearpod Library.

How to Search for Lessons

Once you have logged into your Nearpod account as a teacher, you will have a black navigational window appear on the left side of your screen. Stroll down to *subheading titles* Nearpod Content. Under this heading, you will find the **Nearpod Library**. Once you click on Nearpod Library, it will take you to the search tools for discovering lessons.

You will have a few ways to conduct your searches. You can conduct a search using any of the following methods: Search by standards for core subjects from your state; search by keyword to get a variety of related lessons; search by publisher to get content you know and trust; search by lessons to see lessons by grouped topics; or search by videos to see videos by publisher and grouped topics.

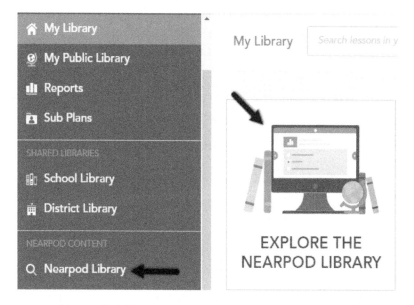

Figure 5-1 Two ways to locate Nearpod Library

As a beginner user, I suggest starting with lessons that are aligned to your state standards, so that you can quickly start using the lessons for digital instruction, as opposed to trying to determine which lessons align or not. So, let's walk through the steps to finding a standard based lesson for a 6th grade Math in the state of Florida.

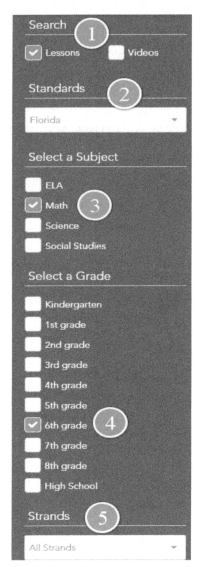

Figure 5-2 Library search tool

1. Check the Lessons box—this will only return lessons in your search.

2. Check the State of Florida for Standards.

3. Check the Math box—this will only return Math lessons.

4. Check the 6th grade box—this will only return 6th grade lessons. as Some lessons will also return within a grade range versus just one grade level. A grade band of 4th -6th could also be beneficial in getting different tiers of mathematical sequence of the lesson.

5. Once you click the grade, the Strand Tab will open. This will allow you to select the math standard for your search.

48

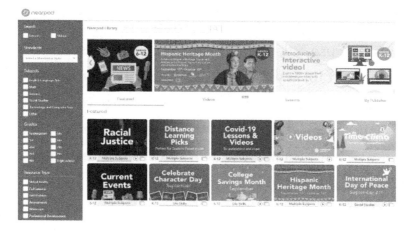

Figure 5-3 Nearpod Library

Figure 5-4 Sample Preview Lesson

After following those steps, you will see lessons populate on the right side of your screen. Click on the lesson that you want to explore further. Once you click on it, you will be taken to a new window where you will then preview the lesson. Consider previewing lessons to determine if it has the content you want and whether it will meet your instructional goals. After previewing, decide on the lesson you want to use. Click on the icon under the lesson that says **Add to My Library**. Then, click **Show in My Library,** so that you can easily launch the lesson with your students and more importantly, wield the power to edit the lesson. There will be a small **Edit** icon under your lesson. This is where you can edit your lesson.

This is but one way to search. Sometimes, there may not be a lesson for your specific state standard. When this happens, the best method to use is to search by keyword. This will allow a variety of related lessons to appear. The next step is to preview the content and determine what pieces of the lesson can work for your instructional needs. You may discover a great way to hook your students into the topic or a stimulation that can be modified to meet your learning goals. The ideas that you discover may help you customize a lesson that fits what you best need. No lesson is ever *a one size fits all.* As a virtual teacher, you will need to adjust a lesson to better meet your students where they are. You will want to edit the lesson 90% of the time. We will discuss how to edit lessons in the next section.

Figure 5-5 Edit feature is starred.

HOW TO CUSTOMIZE LESSONS FROM THE

NEARPOD LIBRARY

The first step to customizing a lesson, is to click on the **Edit** icon. A window will pop up, asking you whether you want to duplicate the lesson or not. I always recommend duplicating the lesson so that if you accidently delete a content slide you can go back to the original lesson to copy it back into the lesson that you are editing. Let's highlight some of her editing features in Nearpod. The first one is the delete option. By clicking on a slide, the **delete tab** in the top bar will be enabled. Once you click on delete, the slide will no longer appear in your lesson.

Figure 5-6 Highlight Slide then Delete Slide

You can also add more content or another activity to your lesson by clicking on the **plus sign,** which is the **Add Slide** button. The window below will show, after which you can choose what feature you would like to add to the lesson.

Figure 5-7 Content Features to Add

Figure 5-8 Activity Features to Add

You can also click on a feature already in the lesson and adjust Poll questions, Quiz questions, Open-Ended Questions, or even Draw It directions. Simply click on the question to delete the text and add the question text that you want. The next way to customize the lesson is to add your voice to content slides. This is even more powerful for lessons that students will access on their own. With this, you can take any content slide and easily add your voice or any mp3 recording to the slide. You need to click on a slide that has content. Once you click it, at the bottom left corner, you will see the **Audio** icon.

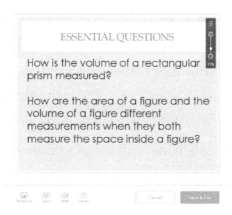

On clicking the Audio icon, two options will be provided, for you to add your audio to the slide. First, you can upload an mp3 file. This is a great option if you want to add music to help students concentrate more on the content they are reading or reflecting on. It is also great if used as a brain break to re-energize their focus on challenging content. The other option is the Audio Recorder, which allows you to record through a microphone, directly from your computer, without any outside software or program. It will also connect you to audio recorder services to hire if you do not wish to record your own voice. This tool is powerful for restating directions, offering feedback on an activity that was previously assigned, or for teaching the lesson.

Sometimes, you may want to alter content on a content slide. The slides have been converted to image files, so you will not be able to directly adjust text on a ready-made lesson. Instead, you can change the layout of the slide by adding an additional content box and/ or title to the slide. This will allow you to adjust what part of the image is showing on the slide. In the image example, you have four possible ways to layout your content. This allows you to add a unit and lesson number attached to the lesson. This allows you to add your name, your period, or more specific information to the slide. It also allows you to add more content formats such as video, gif, or image to the slide layout. You can also remove content publishers' names from your slides. This does not infringe on the copyright use of the lesson, because the lesson is used for educational purposes and not used to make a profit. Also, we all know that students are easily distracted when they see other faces or names in our lessons, and we do not want to increase any possible distractions. I always edit a content slide so that the publisher name does not appear in the slide. Be sure to always click **Save & Exit** to ensure your edits were saved.

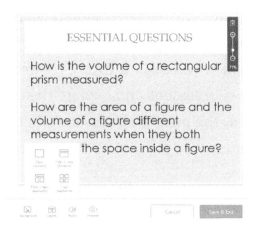

Sometimes, you may come across content slides that you want to convert to a Draw It for your lesson. Simply click on the slide you want to convert, and the convert to Draw It tab at the top of the screen will be enabled. Just click convert Draw It. It will ask you where you want to keep the content slide or if you want to just keep the convert slide. Depending on your situation, you may want to keep it to explain what the next activity will be, or you may choose to have the student go directly to the activity without explaining. It is your choice and it will vary, depending on your learning goal.

One thing to keep in mind is that you have full range to adjust, delete, and add features to the lesson as you deem necessary. This power to edit where you deem fit is another reason why creating virtual learning lessons becomes so much more efficient with ready-made lessons. There are few tools that give teachers the power to customize lessons so easily the way Nearpod does. Once those lessons are customized, you can easily present them or even download a pdf copy of it. This makes adding lesson content to Learning Management Systems easier—you could even add a file to an email or website for future references. The more you customize your lessons and explore the editing features within Nearpod, the more your lessons will be transformed for your students.

KEY POINT

Nearpod offers ready-made lessons and videos that make customizing your lessons efficient and more effective. In a short period of time, you can access research-based instructional lessons with intentional, metacognitive reflections and embedded questioning that lines up to Bloom's Taxonomy, without feeling overwhelmed. Deciding on whether to adjust a little or a lot depends on your learning goal and the needs of your students. With just a little practice, the ability to customize Nearpod lessons will become a permanent skill set for you.

In the next chapter, we will explore how to create your own lessons, using the power of Google Slides.

CHAPTER SIX: USING GOOGLE SLIDES TO CREATE YOUR OWN LESSONS

Imagination is everything. It is the preview of life's coming attractions. -**Albert Einstein**

Google Slides is a presentation tool that is part of a free web-based software office suite program offered by Google. If you team teach, Google Slides lets you view and edit slides from any browser, making it easy to develop content with a team teacher without being physically present. Since many teachers already use Google Slides to make content for their classroom lessons it is an added benefit that Nearpod has a plugin, available with all paid Nearpod subscriptions, that allows you to develop your visually appealing content but have the option to add interactive features to your presentation. In this section, we will review some differences between Google Slides and PowerPoint, how to install the Nearpod add-on, and some advantages from using this tool in your lessons.

WHY GOOGLE SLIDES VERSUS POWERPOINT?

There are seven reasons why Google Slides works better for remote educators. Let's discuss each reason below.

- **Reason #1**: You can access your presentations from any computer or mobile device, making it easy to make edits on the go.
- **Reason #2**: It is a free application, unlike PowerPoint which is a paid application.
- **Reason #3**: Your presentation will look and act the same way on any device.
- **Reason #4**: Easily export and import graphics, text formats, PDFs, or even PowerPoint without a headache.
- **Reason #5**: Easily share the content from your lessons with students via a simple link or in your Google classroom.
- **Reason #6**: Use a ready-made template for your lessons or create visually appealing slides from scratch.
- **Reason #7**: Google Slides offers a Nearpod add-on and PowerPoint does not. This is going to make using Nearpod easier for you and allow you to feel less overwhelmed if you already use it to create your content lessons.
- **Reason #8:** Nearpod's Immersive Reader can easily take text that is typed into your Google Slide and have the text read to the student when this feature is enabled in your lesson settings. Also, this feature can also have the text translated into one

of 100 languages while students are experiencing the lesson.

THE NEARPOD ADD-ON

Now that we know some of the reasons to use Google Slides, let's discuss how to install the Nearpod Add-on. Keep in mind that this add-on is available to teachers with a paid Nearpod license. If you're using the free version of Nearpod, you can still upload your Google Slides and create lessons within the platform.

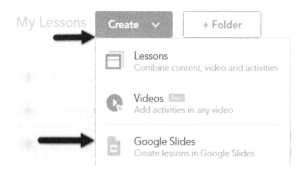

Figure 6-1 Locate Google Slides App

After logging into your Nearpod account, click on the **Lesson** in Google Slides. It will prompt you to login into your Google Account, connecting you to the slides feature.

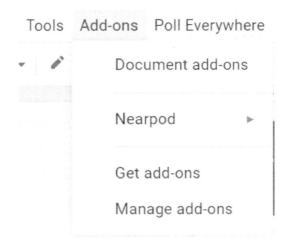

Figure 6-2 Add-on Nearpod App

Instructions will automatically be shown on the Google Slides. But I will walk you through it here too.

1. Click on Add-ons and then Click Get add-ons.
2. Search for Nearpod. Install the Add-on.
3. Once it is installed, you will come back to click on Add-ons. Click on Nearpod and then Open Nearpod.
4. The Nearpod features will open for you on the right slide of the screen.

There is a short video on the top that says *Learn how to use our add-on.* This is a great place to visit if you need a refresher. It is best practice to already have your Google Slide designed with all your content before adding the Nearpod features. These features include Audio, BBC Video, Collaborate Board, Draw It, VR Field Trips, Flocabulary, Fill in the Blank, Flipgrid, Matching Pairs, Graphing Calculator, Nearpod 3-D, Memory Test, Open Ended Question, PDF

Viewer, Poll, Quiz, PhET Simulation, Slideshow, Sway, Time to Climb, Video, and Web Content. We will discuss each feature in more detail in Chapter 11.

Figure 6-3 Nearpod App Features in Slides

Once you decide on the features you want to add to the lesson, click on the feature and follow the prompts to enter or search for the content or activity you will add. You will need to click Save and Go to Nearpod to preview how the feature will be seen by your students. You will not be able to see a preview of the feature inside of the Google Slides program.

When you want to edit your Google Slide, you can log right into your Google Slides and make edits to the text or graphics, without being logged into your Nearpod Account. However, if you want to make changes to Nearpod features, you will need to login into your Nearpod account and click on the Lessons in Google Slides icon. This will log you back into your Google Slides account. Go to Add-ons and click on Nearpod, click on **Open Nearpod,** so that you can edit the features you made or add more features.

One key thing to remember if you decide to present directly from Google Slides is, your Nearpod features will not function if you share the presentation through a link or click the Present button within the Google Slides program. You must always launch the lesson from your Nearpod Account for the features to function properly.

▶ Present ▾

KEY POINT

Google Slides integrates seamlessly with the Nearpod add-on. This add-on gives you the power to create visually appealing lessons with your own text and graphics, enabling the Immersive Reader function to read or translate text for your students. Lastly, you get the interactive features of Nearpod without compromising your creativity. Nearpod is the easiest tool to integrate with other programs you already feel confident using. This sets Nearpod apart from other Edtech tools available for teachers.

In the next chapter, we will discuss how to design virtual lessons that meet your learning goal and the unique needs of a remote learner.

CHAPTER SEVEN: LESSON PLAN DESIGN

A good plan implemented today is better than a perfect plan implemented tomorrow. – **George Patton**

One thing to know about virtual teaching and learning is, it does not have to be boring. It can be very engaging if a lesson is crafted the right way. One rule of thumb used in planning virtual lessons is to make them short and sweet and to always build in-time, for students to have a choice of how they practice or enhance the learning goal more. The idea of creating a 30-minute lesson is ideal, in addition to providing 10 minutes for differentiation and 3-5 minutes to answer questions or direct students to assignments. Each lesson is designed to be only 45 minutes in length.

THE 30-MINUTE LESSON

My 30-minute lesson consists of the following components: Problem of the Day/ Poll Question (2-3 minutes); Inquiry Task and Discussion (8-10 minutes); Direct Instruction (5 minutes); Practice (7 minutes); Checking for Understanding (5 minutes); Differentiation Option (8-10 minutes); and Assignments/Homework for next class (2-3 minutes).

Let's break down each component of the lesson and what features in Nearpod that can support this component.

1. The Problem of the day, a Poll, or an Open-Ended Question aims at getting students to think about today's learning goal. This allows students to log into the Nearpod Lessons and have a task to work on immediately, while they wait for class to start. I would even encourage my students to login into class 5 minutes before the scheduled time, so that they have time to complete their Problem of the day or your Poll Question. One purpose of this task is to also activate their prior knowledge and determine what students already know about the content before teaching it. It also can help you determine if you may need to substitute a lesson for an intervention lesson if most of the students are unable to answer the question correctly. It allows you to call on a student who answered it correctly to explain their thinking to the class before exploring the topic in more detail. This serves to automatically kick off engagement in the day's lesson.

   Nearpod features that support this include the Quiz tool, the Polling Tool, or even the Open-Ended Question tool. You may want to attach an audio file so that they can play meditation music to help facilitate their thinking. The Polling and Open-

Ended Question Tool allow you to add a reference file.

2. Inquiry Task and Discussion purpose is to make your lesson student-centered and allow for students to think. The students should be working within a small group to develop possible approaches to a problem, to generate ideas about a problem; to research a topic, illustrate a problem, or use a virtual stimulation to create possible outcomes for a problem or issue.

   Inquiry tasks are usually open-ended and allow for multiple perspectives and approaches to the problem or issue. Groups do not contain more than 5 people. Products like Zoom allow you to create breakout rooms for your students to complete the tasks. Students are usually given 5-7 minutes to develop their possible outcomes and share their approaches as a whole group with the teacher facilitating the discussion, to help clarify and refine student's thinking. There should be a short summary of the approaches presented by the teacher before going into direct instruction.

Nearpod's **Draw It** feature, allows you to easily collect each group's written responses and even have each student type or write in different colors to support what their contributions were. With this feature, you can upload an image or PDF and students would write or use the text tool to complete the task. In the Draw It feature you can add a reference file, and this can include a website, a PDF to view, a video or audio instructions.

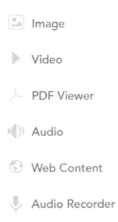

Figure 7 -1 Draw It reference media

The ability to add a reference empowers students to be independent and to learn how to use resources to develop their thinking. Students would review the attached reference resource to help them complete the inquiry task they have. An added benefit of the Draw It feature is that it has a timer. This timer will serve to keep the students on task and provide a reminder of the limited time they have to complete the task. These tasks are designed to focus more on the process than coming up with a correct answer. They are also designed to be open ended so that students try to determine the best way to approach the task.

Two more features to support this task if used for a math or science topic is the Desmos Graphing Calculator and/ or the PhET Simulations. PhET simulations are ready to use, game-like stimulations where students can explore and discover connections through play. These simulations are highly effective when incorporated into your math and science lessons and put into three categories: Elementary, middle school, and high school. In the Desmos graphing calculator, you have blank graphs and premade graphs to help support middle and high school math or provide powerful physics inquiry labs. The goal is for students to build their understanding of complex concepts by having concrete manipulations to explore and test. Your students will make more connections with content presented, when these features are implemented. The premade graphs help students have a starting point and students can input values into variables and see the effect these values have on their respective graphs. The graphs are organized by these categories: Linear, Inequalities, Quadratics, Trigonometry, transformations, Conic Sections, Polar and Parametric, Calculus, Probability and Statistics, and Modeling.

Two more features to support the inquiry task is Flocabulary and/ or VR Field Trips. Flocabulary uses animated hip-hop videos to promote literacy in all four core content areas. Students can review the video as a whole class and pause at key points to highlight key vocabulary terms. It can also be played by a whole class, in which you can have them create a rap, a story, or plot that incorporate key terms repeated in the video. The possibilities to what you want them to create as a result of reviewing the video are open. VR Field Trips are a good way to incorporate historical places into literature or focus on a social issue from social studies. Nearpod has partnered with 360 cities to offer virtual tours for many cities and places in the World. Given a good driving question, students can explore these places or cities to develop possible reasons why certain events took place in history or discuss ways these settings help shape a story or even a revolution. VR Field Trips help put students into their content areas and make easier, real-world connections to topics discussed in class.

Direct Instruction is where the primary focus of the lesson is to teach new content. As a teacher, you will make a direct connection between what students completed in the inquiry tasks and how it relates to the learning goal of the day. This component of the lesson can be your content from your Google Slide, or you can insert a slide from within your Nearpod lesson. It is a good rule of thumb to limit the number of slides to 2 – 4; this will help you stay within the 5-minute window. Another tool to use is the web content feature. This feature always allows you to share a website link without students needing to leave the Nearpod lesson. You may also use it to demo a stimulation site, demo research skills, or explore a site that students may explore for independent practice time or to help teach a concept.

The Practice component can involve either independent or partner practice. Students will have the opportunity to apply the new content taught during direct instruction. Nearpod features that support; this include the Slideshow, Draw-It, PhET Simulations, Desmos Graphing calculator, Fill in the Blank, Open-Ended Question, or a Quiz. Let's discuss some new features mentioned here. Slideshow allows you to insert a mini slide show that focuses on reading a task and perhaps responding to the task in a Google Doc or on a Google Form. It could be students reviewing already solved math problems and pointing out common mistakes they noticed in the problems. Students may complete a Fill in the Blank that focuses on a key concept taught during direct instruction. It may also be used to recall vocabulary terms—if this was tied to the goal of the lesson. A Quiz may be used for students to practice answering questions of a formative assessment. Although it says Quiz, I ensure that my students know that these are practice tools used to give them immediate feedback in a lesson and that it will not be graded. When it is an official grading tool, be sure to label a content slide, to ensure students know the difference.

Check for Understanding is designed to see what students learned in the lesson. It is a 2-4 question formative assessment that is administered using the Quiz tool. It can also be a few, Open-Ended Questions that students respond to. I purposefully used the Quiz tool, so that I can share the results with the class, and they can see what areas they may need to revisit during our differentiation time. They are designed to be short but align with the learning goal of the lesson. Based on the data from this formative assessment three differentiated options are provided for students to explore.

Differentiation Options are provided so that students can be challenged based on their level of understanding. Three options are provided: Challenge Lesson, Practice More Lesson, or Reteach Lesson. You can either assign students to different lessons or you can allow the students to choose the lesson they want to do. Each lesson will be a link to a new Nearpod lesson that should take the students about 8 minutes to complete on their own. The best way to provide the three-lesson links is to create a Google Docs, title each lesson and insert a link for each title. Once you have completed this, you will get the shared link and add it to your 30-minute lesson as a Web content feature. This option will be discussed further in the next chapter, which covers how to create these three types of lessons more in-depth.

Assignments and/or Homework is used to extend the learning of the lesson. There are several ways to do this:

1. You may just make an announcement of what assignments they must complete.
2. You may create a content slide that has homework posted.

3. You may already be using a Learning Management System like Google Classroom or Canvas and direct students to check their assignments there.

4. You may provide a PDF that students need to download to their computers, complete and upload to an email or other means to send it back to you.

This completes the basic components of a 30-minute lesson. If done correctly, your number of content slides are reduced to less than 10 slides. This is ideal for a virtual teacher, as the goal is for students to be on an academic task for most of the lesson and help increase their academic engagement.

SAMPLE LESSON PLAN

Math Lesson on the Pythagorean Theorem for 8th Grade

Learning Goal: Students can prove the Pythagorean Theorem by using triangles and squares and apply this understanding to solve right triangle problems that have a missing side.

Problem of the Day: Find the Square of each of these numbers: 5, 8, 12, and 10. Use the Open-Ended feature to collect responses quickly and assess student prior knowledge.

Inquiry Tasks and Discussion: How can we prove the Pythagorean Theorem?

Given this right triangle, find the side lengths of each side and the areas of each side. Write at least 1 pattern you notice between the squares and side lengths.

Discussion Questions: What objects resemble a right triangle in the real world? What are some reasons why a person may want to find the missing side of a triangle? Use the one content slide to introduce the task and the Draw It feature, for student responses to be collected in real time.

Direction Instruction: Play Nearpod Original Interactive Video Pythagorean Theorem 4 minutes with embedded student questions and whole group discussion of their responses. Use the Interactive Video feature in Nearpod.

Independent or Partner Practice: Provide another example of cube inquiry task, a problem with one missing side, and a problem with hypotenuse missing. Use the Draw It feature for students to practice writing the steps of the problem and see if students have any gaps in completing the tasks. Even while working with a partner, students should also submit their own written work.

Check for Understanding: Provide 2-word problems with one missing side, missing vocabulary term in a comprehension sentence, and one problem with hypotenuse missing. Use the Quiz tool to get responses immediately. Use the Quiz tool to get a quick assessment score to easily assign students to their designated differentiated lessons.

Differentiation Option: Use the Nearpod lesson Prove the Pythagorean Theorem Using Squares and Triangles by LearnZillion and adjust it to meet these three lesson types: Challenge, Practice, and Reteach lesson.

Challenge lesson is for students who score 90% or higher on Check for Understanding:

Use slides 8, 15, & 16 and add a Draw It where students create their own example of the Pythagorean Theorem using a right triangle. Provide answer explanations using the audio recorder to provide student feedback at the end of the lesson.

Practice lesson is for students who score 70% to 90% on Check for Understanding:

Use slides 7-10, 14 and add a Draw It with two problems to solve.

Reteach lesson is for students who score less than 69% on Check for Understanding:

Use slides 4-8, 9, 12-13 (embedded video from LearnZillion found on the first slide and play before inserting the recommended slides) and use the audio recorder to explain each content slide. Provide an overview of the correct responses at the end of the lesson.

You are expected to add the lesson to your library and duplicate the lesson each time you want to adjust the content of it. You need to select the slides you want to delete and add the needed features that may be missing from the existing lesson.

Homework: Provide a link to an assignment from the assigned textbook, online Learning Management System, or an assignment created by you using Google Forms or Microsoft Forms.

Use the Web content feature to get the link for your created Google Docs that has a link to each of the three lessons. Provide instructions there on which lesson a student should select for this activity.

To get a digital copy of this lesson—with digital links to the reference lesson—please visit the Resources section of this book.

English Language Arts lesson on Persuasive Writing for 5th grade.

Learning Goal: Students can brainstorm, create, and identify persuasive writing samples that move a person to take action using simple sentence structures.

Open Ended Question: What are some synonyms for the word persuade? Use any resource to help you answer this question.

Inquiry Task and Discussion Questions: Go on a VR Reality Tour of a Tree House using the Nearpod lesson Persuasive Writing Practice: Tree House using slides 1, 4-7, have students work with a partner to develop three reasons why or why they would not live in a tree house. Type their responses using the Open-Ended feature. Review responses to highlight students with strong evidence versus those with weak evidence.

Direction Instruction: Use Nearpod lesson Persuasive Writing: Unusual Homes slides 6-8, 10-12.

Practice: Write a paragraph of at least 4 sentences, highlighting two benefits of living in the house from the video. Include persuasive words that would make a person want to live in that house.

Check for Understanding: Create a Quiz that has students identify the correct persuasive sentences from sample multiple choice sentences (at least 3 questions). Provide one question with a persuasive paragraph and have students identify the key reasons it is persuasive from a multiple-choice list.

Differentiation Options: Use two different Nearpod lessons to create your Challenge and Reteach lesson and use the video from your lesson to create the Practice lesson.

Challenge lesson: Use Nearpod Lesson The Power of Persuasion, slides 4-12. Revise the open-ended question to ensure they are individual activities.

Practice lesson: Provide at least two sentence starters and have students write a paragraph on why they would not want to live in the unusual home featured in the video. Provide the video link so students can review the video on their own.

Reteach lesson: Review the Nearpod lesson writing paragraphs, adjust the content slides so that it is an independent practice using slides 6-9, 11-13. Please, use the audio recorder to provide instructions and explain each activity.

Assignment: Students will create a persuasive letter to help more students attend their live virtual lessons as opposed to watching the recording of the lesson. The letter should include an opening statement, three convincing reasons, and a closing statement. This assignment can be given in your Learning Management System or with a link to a Google Doc that they will copy and submit to you when it is completed.

Hopefully, these sample lesson plans have given you a taste of how using the Nearpod Library can help you create effective lessons that meet the unique needs of your learners and help you plan lessons that help students think and construct long lasting connections to academic content. To get a digital copy of this lesson—with digital links to the reference lesson, please visit oliviaodileke.com/lessons.

KEY POINT

By following the 30-minute lesson template, you create lessons that help students stay on task longer and promote higher order thinking. By utilizing Nearpod features, creating a 30-minute lesson will require less time and increase your efficiency as a teacher. These include lessons that focus on students using their critical thinking skills, working with partners, and having opportunities to explore content based on their readiness. These methods of lesson planning will help you transform your virtual teaching to another level and your students will appreciate you more for it. Use it and you will make lesson planning one of the joys of your profession.

CHAPTER EIGHT: DIFFERENTIATE YOUR LESSONS

He who stops being better stops being good. –
Oliver Cromwell

Instructions must meet the needs of each student. This means that instruction is not identical for all students. To ensure equity for students, our lessons require appropriate accommodations to promote access for all students. Differentiate benefits students by making learning more relevant, motivating students to stay more engaged, and students experience more success when learning takes place in their zones of proximal development. The goal is to implement instruction that meets the varied needs of students.

Hence, what is differentiation, and what is the easiest and fastest way to do it? Differentiation means tailoring instruction to meet individual needs. Teachers have the option to differentiate by content, process, or products, but it should include the use of ongoing assessment and flexible grouping to make this instructional approach successful. There are three main instructional areas that you can adjust to meet the needs of your learners:

- Content—the knowledge and skills students need to master.

- Process—the activities students use to master the content.
- Product—the method students use to demonstrate learning.

When creating your whole group Nearpod lessons, it is critical that you appeal to the three types of learning styles: visual, audio, and kinesthetic. These will be a great starting point to differentiating your content. This will help students to retain the information more by differentiating the content with these three learning styles in mind. Here are examples of Nearpod features for each learning style that can be incorporated into your lessons.

Audio Strategies: Audio files can be added to any content slide and be replayed for repetition. Immersive Reader can be enabled to have text read to students and even translated to over 100 languages.

Visual Strategies: Use slideshows, virtual reality tours, videos, reference images for visual support, bold graphics, different text colors, and 3D images.

Kinesthetic Strategies: Students benefit from learning by doing. Nearpod features that support kinesthetic learners include: Open-Ended Questions, Poll, Draw It, Matching Pairs, VR Field Trips, 3D images, Google Education suite tools, and collaborating.

The next step is to differentiate your lessons by process. This step helps to personalize the learning more and will provide the needed rigor for the student proximity of learning to flourish. The goal is to create a 10-minute differentiated lesson primarily based on Nearpod extensive ready-to-use lesson library. I primarily create three different mini lessons to meet the individual needs of my students. Typically, this mini lesson is administered after students complete a 2-4 question Check for Understanding assessment. I can assign the students the lesson by a percentage they received on the assessment, and I would have a Google Docs created with a link to each mini-lesson and a score range for which one to choose. I can equally review the scores and assign the lessons verbally or by assigning in class using Google Classroom or another Learning Management System. You have choices, so choose the one that is easiest for you.

Each lesson is created to incorporate one of Bloom's taxonomy learning targets. The easiest way to differentiate the process is to use Nearpod's Library to access ready-made lessons. Usually, I can take a standard-based lesson and adjust the lesson to create three mini-lessons. You should focus on the verbs in the question types presented in the Nearpod Lessons to adjust the lesson. You only include the verbs that align to Bloom's taxonomy for that lesson type and delete any questions or activities that do not align. I will provide an example of each type of lesson and how this might be used in each of the core subject areas.

CHALLENGE LESSON

The purpose of a challenge lesson is for students to evaluate the academic content and/or create a product based on the content presented. These may include providing an extended quiz that provides more real world scenarios and asked for the student to evaluate the best possible outcome, providing articles or website links where students are asked to read and respond to an article or problem and provide evidence to support their thinking or claim, or creating a product that demonstrates mastery of the topic. Let's look at a standard for each core subject area and provide examples of how the lesson could be differentiated.

SOCIAL STUDIES EXAMPLE: 7TH GRADE

SS.7.C.3.1 Compare different forms of government (direct democracy, representative democracy, socialism, communism, monarchy, oligarchy, autocracy).

As you evaluate the world map and types of governments in the map, what trends did you notice?

Lesson requires students to evaluate possible reasons certain types of governments exist in different parts of the world. This lesson extends the learning goal of the lesson.

Math Example: 4th

MAFS.4.MD.1.3 Apply the area and perimeter formulas for rectangles in real world and mathematical problems.

Have students solve real world word problems and create their own perimeter and area problems for students to solve.

Lesson requires students to apply their knowledge of perimeter and area and extend it by creating their own problems.

Language Arts Example: 6th Grade

LAFS.6.RL.4.10 By the end of the year, read and comprehend literature, including stories, dramas, and poems, in the grades 6–8 text complexity band proficiently, with scaffolding as needed at the high end of the range.

Provide a Poem and have students respond to these questions. What did the repetition, rhyme, and alliteration make you think of? How does the sound impact the poem? Does it support or contrast with the poem's overall feeling? Explain how repetition, rhyme, and alliteration can impact a reader's emotions.

Lesson requires the student to respond to several open-ended questions and requires the student to evaluate their understanding of each of the three terms and its role in impacting the reader's emotions.

SCIENCE EXAMPLE: 8TH GRADE

SC.8.P.9.2 Differentiate between physical changes and chemical changes.

Review images of physical and chemical changes identify the correct change and include a brief reason to support their answer. Or, students can create a Fryer Model, given key vocabulary terms, as well as examples and non-examples of both chemical and physical changes.

Lesson requires students to evaluate what makes a physical and chemical change. Students must support their explanation. This lesson extends the learning by allowing students to create a graphic organizer to solidify their understanding of the two types of changes.

PRACTICE LESSON

The purpose of a practice lesson is for students to apply and analyze the academic content presented. Students need to build context and demonstrate comprehension of the content presented. These lessons may include reviewing vocabulary terms, practicing more problems, further analysis of a topic by drawing conclusions among ideas, or applying a concept in a new situation. We will look at the same standards from the Challenge lesson and adjust it to become a Practice lesson.

Social Studies Example: 7th Grade SS.7. C.3.1

Define communism and describe at least 3 of its features. Provide content slides or a short video on communism.

Math Example: 4th Grade MAFS.4.MD.1.3

Have students solve perimeter and area problems by excluding one of the variables. Provide pictures for students to label the sides before applying the formula.

Language Arts Example: 6th Grade LAFS.6.RL.4.10

Review a poem and highlight examples of repetition, rhyme, and alliteration in the poem. Use the Draw It feature with the poem as the background for each example. Teacher provides an exemplary response after the student completes their own example first. Provide at least two poems to complete this exercise with.

Science Example: 8th Grade SC.8. P.9.2

Provide a reference image showing the changes of water. Have students respond to these questions. Let's investigate the changes in states of water by analyzing the reference image. What is the change from a gas to a liquid called? What kind of change is this? An example is for students to complete a Fill in the Blank that focuses on key ideas presented throughout the lesson.

These examples focus on allowing the student more time to practice applying the knowledge gain in the lesson and reinforce their understanding of the topic.

RETEACH LESSON

The focus of a reteach lesson is for students to remember, recall, and to understand the academic content presented. Some example of this include: Reviewing a video and answering embedded questions, to gear their comprehension on the information presented; reviewing the basic steps to a problem and being asked to list the steps in chronological order; reviewing vocabulary and understanding their meaning in different scenarios; or retelling a story in their own words. The key idea is that a reteach is focused on helping the student to recall key information presented in the lesson and for them to get a basic understanding of the topic.

Social Studies Example: 7th Grade SS.7. C.3.1

Review a short video and respond to this question. In your own words, define fascism and totalitarianism.

Math Example: 4th Grade MAFS.4.MD.1.3

Review area and perimeter formulas. Provide examples of area and perimeter. Have students generate examples of each. Have students write the formula on their own and point to an image example of area and match the correct formula to it.

Language Arts Example: 6th Grade LAFS.6.RL.4.10

Define repetition and give an example. Define rhyme and give an example. Define alliteration and give an example.

<u>Science Example: 8th Grade SC.8. P.9.2</u>

Provide a video that discusses physical and chemical changes with examples. Have students write the examples and label whether the example is a physical or a chemical change.

Reteach lessons focus on students recalling key information in terms of math formulas, vocabulary terms, or basic ideas in the topic.

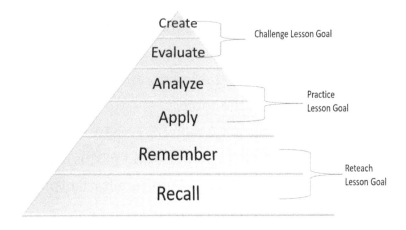

Figure 8 Differentiation Lesson Pyramid based on Bloom's Taxonomy

KEY POINT

Differentiation is easier when you can access ready-made lessons in the Nearpod Library and adjust the lesson to create a Challenge, Practice, or Reteach lesson. Each lesson's purpose is based on meeting your learners where they are. If a student shows mastery on their Check for

Understanding assessment, then provide a Challenge lesson so they can further evaluate or create products that extend their learning. If a student obtains a passing score between your designated ranges, then provide a Practice lesson so they can further apply their knowledge to build their confidence through practice. And lastly, if a student fails a Check for Understanding assessment, provide the Student a Reteach lesson so that they can remember and recall the basic concepts previously presented in the lesson. Sometimes, this group benefits more from repetition.

These lessons can be easily assigned during a live lesson by creating a Google Docs, adding the hyperlinks to each lesson and inputting the Google Docs link as a Web content in your Nearpod lesson. By doing this additional step, you can easily incorporate differentiated instruction options without spending hours planning for it. (An example is provided under Resources.)

CHAPTER NINE: LAUNCHING YOUR VIRTUAL LESSONS

Everything you want is just outside your comfort zone. - **Robert Allen**

We have discussed ways to create engaging and student-centered lessons, now let's shift the discussion to ways you can launch the lesson with your students. All lessons must be launched by the teacher in order to generate access to the lesson by students. You can think of it as launching your PowerPoint presentation, by clicking the Slide Show tab or launching your Google Slide presentation by clicking the Present button. This action puts your presentation in full screen mode, ready for presentation. This same concept can be applied to launching your Nearpod lesson. Let's discuss three ways to launch a lesson and suitable times to use each method.

LIVE PARTICIPATION

When launching a Live Participation lesson, the teacher controls the pace of the lesson. As a teacher, you can control what slide is being displayed to all your students. You can view the progress of a student in real time, when completing a Draw It. This is powerful in providing information in the moment of engagement and whether a student is completing the task. Live participation is most ideal when students are in a live online session through your designated web conferencing tool.

To launch a Live Participation session, you just hover over the lesson in your Nearpod Library and click the Live Participation button. A box will pop up with a five-character session code, containing letters and numbers. This code can be shared for students to enter, by going to join.nearpod.com. After entering the code, it will prompt the student to enter their name and click on the *join session* button to enter your lesson. This is one way to enter the session and it is recommended for older students or students who have been trained in this process and feel comfortable with it. Under the five-digit code, you are presented with other ways to share your code. The two best ways for a Live Participation lesson is to generate a link that can be shared in the chat box of your video conferencing program or to have it added to your Google Classroom. If you click the Google Classroom tab, you will be directed to login to your Google account and select the course you want to add the link to. When you generate a link, a small box will pop up with the link, which you can easily copy and paste as a word document, to be shared with students via the chat box. This facilitates easy access during the lesson.

Live Participation links are only active for 14 days. Beware of this, if you decide to add it to your Google Classroom as opposed to sharing it as a link in the chat box.

If you launch the lesson, but do not want to teach at that moment, you can choose to end the lesson but with the option to resume it later. When you are ready to teach it, click Live Participation and the previous code generated will be highlighted. If you click the previous code, it will ask you if you want to resume the lesson. Be sure to say Yes, so that you do not need to generate another code.

When launching a Student-Paced lesson, the student is in control of the pace of the lesson. These types of lessons are best used for tutorials, flipped lessons, differentiate lessons, and even virtual newsletters for parents. One advantage of a Student-Paced lesson is the generated code can be used for up to 1 year from the date you launch it. You as a teacher can set a date for when the code expires, but it can only be up to one year. An efficient feature of a self-paced lesson is the teacher's ability to view progress in real time. So, if you administer a differentiate self-paced lesson during a Live Class, you could open another window, find the lesson you want to view, and click on self-paced mode to view progress in real time. You would need to do this for each lesson assigned and simply click view progress. The students who are logged in will be able to see what part of the lesson they have completed and you will even be able to see what parts they may be struggling in.

Figure 9-1 Resume Live Participation Window

You have the same options for generating a code for Student--Paced mode as you have for Live Participation. You may provide the five-digit code and have students enter it at join.nearpod.com. You can generate a code, you can email it, or you can place it as a link in Google Classroom or through your school's LMS, like Canvas or Schoology. If you decided to implement the Differentiate Option component of the Lesson Design Chapter, you will generate a link for each lesson, place it in a Google Docs and click Share to generate a link for your Google Doc. The link will then be placed inside of the Nearpod lesson for students to have easy access to their personalized lesson.

LIVE PARTICIPATION WITH ZOOM

Use this if you want to create a Zoom meeting immediately, without logging into your Zoom account separately. You can still share your screen to broadcast the Nearpod lesson, but you can quickly get a participant link and password to send to your participants. Also, your students will automatically be logged into your Nearpod lesson, so there is no need to generate an additional join session code. To launch this type of lesson, you will click on Live Participation with Zoom, after which you will be given a link and a code for logging into your Nearpod lesson. Under the code, you will see the option to enable your Zoom meeting. When you turn this option on, you will be directed to login into your Zoom account and add Nearpod as an approved app for your Zoom account. After it is approved, you will now be in your Zoom account. Once in the Zoom account, you will still need to share the link to the lesson or provide the five-digit code, have students go to join.nearpod.com and enter the code to participate in the lesson. Students then automatically join the Nearpod lesson and Zoom at the same time, with the waiting room feature automatically enabled. The main advantage of this option is direct login into Zoom, with an invitation link ready to be shared via email, announcement page, or directly into a Learning Management System for instant session participation.

Key Point

Nearpod offers three ways for you to launch your lessons with your students. The Student-Paced option provides a solution allowing students to explore content at their own pace and to provide mini lessons to differentiate the process of the lesson. It is great for tutorials on topics or for content that may need to be reviewed at different durations of time per individual student needs. Live Participation mode is best used in teacher facilitated live lessons where discussions, partnered or group activities are planned during instruction. Lastly, the Live Participation with Zoom allows easy access to creating a Zoom session without leaving the Nearpod platform. The lesson code still needs to be shared for students to participate in the lesson. Each launch serves a different purpose, and this creates flexible lesson delivering options for the virtual teacher.

In the next chapter, we will discuss how to access reports and what information is contained in the reports section.

PART III: USING DATA TO INFORM YOUR PRACTICE

――――――♦◇♦――――――

To help students grow academically, we must first understand where they are and what they need. Nearpod provides various formative assessment and reporting tools to help you in this task. In this section, you want to think about how you can use the Nearpod reporting features to increase the growth of each of your students.

What are the key purposes of having students' complete assessments? What are your beliefs about assessments? Think about why you will use assessments to help drive student growth. Assessments are needed to inform and improve your teaching. Assessments should be an ongoing process that is seamlessly embedded in each lesson. Teachers need multiple data points to construct an accurate picture of what a student knows and can perform. As you think about the purpose of assessments in your virtual classroom, also consider how you will make your classroom more student centered, allowing students time to struggle, get corrective feedback, and to keep trying until they feel confident in their skills.

If one of our primary purposes of assessing students is to inform our instruction and provide opportunities for student growth, then we need interactive assessments that both expose what students know and what they can do independently. Providing more opportunities for students to provide their own ideas, create products, and demonstrate their learning through performance tasks gives more relevance to how Nearpod can be utilized to create those types of opportunities. This will aid teachers in making data relevant and create more data sources to really grasp a student's understanding of the standard.

As you think about the types of data you will gather in your virtual lessons, you want to go beneath the surface with your assessments. Although multiple choice responses or fill in the blanks are easy to grade, they only scratch the surface. For example, think of your content area understanding as an ant hill. The surface of an ant hill represents basic understanding of the content area. The average ant hill may be about a foot in height. But an average ant colony can go as deep as 25 feet under the surface, unbeknownst to the on looker. When assessments go beneath the surface, you can better uncover your students' understanding, by using multiple assessment strategies. Think about how often you want to use assessments that go below the surface of the learning goal. In Nearpod, these strategies include using the Draw It feature, eliciting student understandings with Open-Ended Questions, including the Slideshow feature that provides opportunities for small group discussions, providing reflections with the Flipgrid integration in a lesson, your observations of students completing activities in the Draw It, and the types of questions and responses students may generate on the Collaborate Board.

Hopefully, you will make your beliefs about assessments and data actionable by providing your belief statement below. May it serve as a guide for you, as you create lessons that meet the needs of all your learners and provide multiple assessment opportunities that go beneath the surface to uncover real student understandings.

I believe that assessments are

_____.

CHAPTER TEN: WHAT TO DO WITH REPORTS?

Knowledge is of no value unless you put it into practice.-
Anton Chekhov

Reports are designed to give you a quick overview of how your class performed overall. Nearpod was designed as an interactive presentation and instruction tool. It was not designed as an assessment tool and for the purpose of providing grades every time a student accesses a lesson. It is important that you keep this in mind as you review the reports tab. It is a tool for organically passing across your instruction. It is a powerful, formative assessment tool for giving your multiple assessment points to help you uncover your students' understanding. By reviewing your class lesson reports, it can help you to quickly assess what students know, where the gaps are, and provide the needed intervention for them. If you want to use Nearpod as a summative assessment, it is best practice to set it up as a separate Nearpod lesson, where you only include a direction for the assessment slide and then the quiz. This way, you can quickly get a grade to share to your gradebook. Otherwise, it may be more advantageous to use a Google Form, through which you can include open-ended questions and see all student responses from one spreadsheet, that can easily be scored with an add-on, such as Flubaroo. Flubaroo can be used to grade forms automatically and leave space for you to manually enter a score from open ended responses.

There are two ways to access your Reports. If you finish a Live session, you can have a report emailed directly to you after the session. At the top of the lesson, Nearpod will be in the middle and there is a drop-down box with a **Reports tab**. When you click on Reports, it will ask you to type the email address of where you want to send the report. The other option is to go to your Nearpod dashboard—on the left navigation bar, you can click on **Reports**.

When you land in Reports, you will find a tile image of your lesson—click on it. It will show you the date and time the session began. You need to click on the date and time for the report to populate. Now, we will review the three basic components of the Reports section.

SUMMARY SETTING

Summary provides an overview percentage of students, who participated in all activities in the lesson— what ratio of correct responses where measured on quizzes given, a detailed list of every student who was in the session, each feature they participated in and an overall participation percentage for all features in the lesson. The goal is to have 100% participation from all students in the last row titled **Participation**. This will show that the student attempted the featured activity. This is also a great way to quickly take attendance or provide participation points.

ACTIVITY SETTING

On the left side of Summary, each activity you provided in the lesson will be listed. In the example below, a Quiz, Open-Ended Question, Draw It, and Interactive Video were activities that were added to the lesson. Just click on the activity you want to see more data on—click on Quiz and see a summary tab that shows each question and the percentage of correct answers for that question. A circle graph will show the overall percentage of correct, wrong, or no answer. The next tabs will show each question and the response of each student, plus a summary circle graph of correct, wrong, or no answers. The next feature Open-Ended Question will show their responses and provide a circle graph showing the percentage of No Answer and Free Text. The goal is for Free Text to be 100%, showing that every student created a written or audio response. The Draw It feature will show each Draw It question and each individual student image. Just click the image to enlarge it for reviewing purposes. For the Interactive Video, click on **class board,** which will direct you back to the actual Interactive Video. You will need to click on the blue dots in the video play stream to see each student's response. To recap, each activity that a student participates in will be in the features area. This is an easy way to go back and get a quick overview of how students responded to your activities.

DOWNLOAD OR SHARE OPTIONS

At the top of your Report, you have a Download and a Share option available for your report. Under the Download option, you can download the results as a CSV file, which is compatible with Excel or Google Sheets, to view the data in a numerical format. You will choose where you want the file to download to; either your Local Drive (your computer) or your Google Drive. It will download as a zip file and every Draw It will be saved as an individual jpg file. Students' names and each activity feature will be listed. For the Draw It feature, it will just reference the jpg file name in the zip folder. Each Quiz score will be in an easy to read column and you will have an empty column for entering Open-Ended Questions scores, based on their responses. This data can easily be imported into your grade book to help you track activities you want to count as a grade. It may be helpful to recreate tabs for each period or each subject area, to help you have your data in an easy to read spreadsheet.

You can also download the report as a PDF, but it will look like the Report that populates when you open the report. It will provide a summary, circle graphs, and a feature report with each student's names listed. This is great for a quick visual overview of how the students performed in the lesson. This option is also available for individual student reports. If you click on Student PDFs, you can select all or individual students to see their results in greater detail. These are the types of reports that are easy to share with Parents during Teacher-Parent Conferences and help highlight their effort and thinking in your lessons. You can also get an individual CSV report for students by clicking on CSV student view.

Sharing reports are easy and a great way to collaborate with your Special Education Teacher, an Instructional Coach, a Grade level team, or for a Professional Learning Community (PLC) group. It can be used to highlight sound, instructional practices and a way to reflect with others on the progress of your students. You just need to type in their email address and press send. The respondent will receive a PDF copy of the report with circle graphs included.

All lessons launched as Live Participation, Student-Paced, and Live Participation in Zoom will automatically create a report of the lesson, even if you are disconnected from the lesson. The reports do not have an expiration date. The only way for it to be removed is for you to delete the report. If you launch a lot of sessions, you will need to click the load more button so that more reports can be loaded to your screen. The reports section does not have a folder feature, but Nearpod is always receiving feedback from teachers on how to make the program better. You also have the option to search for a lesson report by Lesson name. This is the easiest way to find an older lesson, if you do not wish to keep pressing the load more button

KEY POINT

Reports give you more in-depth, formative assessment data to determine how students are progressing towards the learning goal. In the virtual classroom, data is a powerful means for quickly adjusting content in order to meet students where they are. This data quickly shows who participated in your activities as well as the quality and depth of their understanding. It is also a great starting point for data chats about individual students with easy to reference graphs and individual student reports. You have two ways of viewing the report—either as a CSV file or a PDF file, depending on your purpose. If you just want a quick visual overview, use the PDF version. If you want to use the lesson as a grade or to collect scores for certain activities, use the CSVS file version. Lastly, sharing a lesson report is easy. Just email the report to whomever you want to share or collaborate with to strengthen your teaching pedagogy. Reports is a powerful tool for a virtual teacher to stay informed on what is helping students to learn and what growth areas there are in a lesson. Use reports to help you grow your craft and proactively respond to the needs and unique circumstances of your students.

In the next chapter, we will highlight the top ten features to use in Nearpod.

Chapter Eleven: Top 10 Features to Use ASAP

Things may come to those who wait, but only things left by those who hustle. -**Abraham Lincoln**

As we have discovered, Nearpod offers many interactive features to help educators increase student engagement and transform their learning experience. Each year, Nearpod adds more features to make it easier for teachers to reach and meet the needs of all learners—tools that cross economic and cultural barriers to unite the learning experience and have students excited to learn again. It is important to highlight some of the distinguishing features that are available and offer some suggested activities to do within these features. Let's review five go-to features under Content and five go-to features under Activities.

Content Features

Interactive Video

The first recommended feature is Interactive Video. Interactive Video allows you to present video content, but to also collect data on what students understand about the content. There are two question types: open-ended and multiple choice. Each question type allows you to collect data in real time and share the responses with all participants. This feature can be used as a standalone lesson or easily integrated with an existing Nearpod lesson. Research also shows that questioning embedded in content videos stimulates more active participation and promotes active student engagement. Using content videos in a virtual class is an essential tool for building active participation and engagement in academic topics. Oftentimes, the deeper levels of discussion are overlooked because it was not initially embedded in the video itself.

There are three types of videos that can be used to make interactive videos. The three types are: Uploading your own video, searching for a YouTube video, or searching the Nearpod library for a video with questions already embedded. When you already have a lesson created, it is easy to add an interactive video to your lesson. Just click on add a slide and choose video under the Content tab. The window below will pop up, giving you three ways to add video to your lesson. The default option is the Nearpod Video Library, where you can search by standard or topic. The YouTube option allows you to search YouTube in the Nearpod interface. Lastly, you can upload an mp4, avi, or mov formatted video and it will be saved to your library for future use.

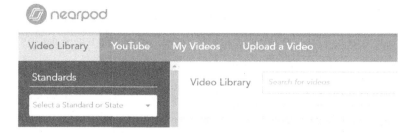

Figure 11-1 Video Library Feature

Slide

To access the slide feature, click on Add a Slide under the Content tab. The Slide feature offers several advantages for a lesson. Let's highlight some of those advantages:

- Any text typed into a slide can be read to students when you enable the Immersive Reader option.
- There are several layout options available and this creates an effective way to differentiate content. For example, you can create a layout with four content areas, and you have the option to add text, an image, gif, or even video, allowing you to create four ways for students to experience the content.
- You can add an audio file or record audio directly to the slide, providing instructions on what students are expected to do while engaging with the content.
- There is the option to add a background to the slide. Images may be searched directly from google, uploaded from your computer or your cloud drive.

- The slide feature is a great way to introduce an activity, video, or a preview of what to expect in a part of the lesson.

Overall, the slide feature makes it easy to add content directly to your slide and incorporate audio for direction or feedback purposes, and to even provide students options on how they engage with the content of the lesson.

Web content

The key function of this feature is to embed website content within your lesson without leaving the Nearpod platform. It reduces transition time in students entering the correct URL for a website resource. It also allows you to easily direct students to Google resources such as docs, forms, or sheets without disturbing the flow of the lesson. Any website's URL can be copied and pasted into the web content tool. This allows the site to seamlessly show within the lesson and have students' complete external tasks, while keeping all your resources in one place.

Slideshow

Slideshow feature allows students to be placed into virtual breakout rooms and have their tasks mapped out in a mini slide show that they can stroll through without the teacher directing the content. It allows an opportunity for students to discuss, read, or share their opinions on topics in a small group. It is usually best practice to have a few groups share out the key points from their group's discussion or summarize the tasks they completed together. It is also a natural pause in the lesson for the teacher to check in with students, who may not be participating in the lesson or to do some housekeeping items with students who are present. The slideshow options work best in Live Participation mode and when students can work in pairs or within a small group, usually no more than 5 students.

VR Field Trip

If you want to bring the world to your classroom, then using the VR Field Trips will be your number one feature. I encourage you to use your imagination with the VR Field Trip feature as it is only limited by your ability to imagine the possibilities. You simply type in a destination, place, or city and it will provide 360-degree images of the location. VR Field Trips work best when used to explore a topic and are used with driving questions that help students use their observation and inference skills to connect concepts and response to questions. This exploration activity serves as a visual motivator and method for engaging students into content and immediately making a real-world connection to the goal of their learning. All ages and academic levels are highly engaged when this tool is provided, in conjunction with driving questions to promote curiosity in the exploration activity.

By incorporating these five features into the content of a lesson, it accelerates their ability to access the academic goal. Each feature compounds the efforts to provide a different lesson that meets the needs of all learners. Videos will meet the needs of the visual and auditory learner especially with embedded questions, which give rise to richer discussion about academic topics. The Slideshow feature helps slow the flow of the lesson and give students time to interact with the content and deepen their understanding, by engaging in conversations about what they are learning. The web content tool may offer digital manipulatives, models, or samples to be shared easily and from a different media or perspective that helps oriented the learner to engage with the content on an easier level or more accessible level. The slide feature gives you another avenue to present the content using text, image, and video—plus the ability to add audio to clarify thoughts and recall previous stated facts or activity directions. Lastly, the VR Field Trips make learning real by affording educators the opportunity to make more connections with tangible places, settings, or buildings.

ACTIVITY FEATURES

The activity features of Nearpod give educators the data necessary to make just-in time informed decisions on what learners need to progress academically to meet the learning goal of a lesson or unit. Every feature in the activity category collects data from each student and stores it in Reports for future review. Let's review five features that will make your lesson more interactive and increase student participation.

Draw It

As a virtual educator, one of our biggest challenges is being able to see what students are working on in a live session in real time. Most educators rely on chat, use of microphones, or students to complete a Google doc or form. Those tools still have limitations, as most of the time we need to see the thinking behind a student's response. Look no further, Draw It allows students to draw, write, type, highlight, and insert images or screenshots. Any paper that could have been copied and distributed to students can now be scanned as a PDF document and uploaded as a background to a Draw It. You can also upload png or jpeg images to use as the background of the tool. Additionally, as students are responding, a teacher can see their progress in real time, prior to the student submitting their final response. This tool gives the virtual teacher a means to be creative with how students demonstrate mastery or practice new skills learned in a lesson. It will be a tool you want to employ in every Nearpod lesson you launch.

Open-Ended Question

In a nutshell, Open-Ended Questions helps educators know what students are thinking in a very powerful and safe way. I always have over 90% of my students respond to my Open-Ended Questions, even if it is to say I do not know, or I do not understand at this time. This is more information than the classroom teacher receives, as he or she is not able to solicit information from each student in a short period of time and still maintain a climate where students feel safe to express their inner thoughts. It is also powerful when they know that their responses are not seen or heard by the whole class. This makes them feel safer to share them directly with the teacher. All their responses are data points for the responsive teacher who is constantly looking for ways to uncover academic topics as opposed to telling students about academic topics. Open-Ended Responses provide the fuel for rigor and increase the Bloom Taxonomy level by allowing more opportunities for students to evaluate and analyze questions, rather than just being asked to remember and recall information. It is highly recommended that Opened-Ended Questions be used to help students evaluate and analyze a topic—not just being used to just recall content presented in a lesson.

Poll Questions

Polls serves as a survey tool for classroom discussions. It can easily be used to activate prior knowledge and inform you about what a student already knows regarding a topic. It is useful as a voting tool on a topic you may want to explore as a class. For example, you can use a poll to see what topic students are interested in the most and thus, provide a choice in what is discussed in class. Nearpod allows you to easily go to any slide during the lesson, without disturbing the flow of the lesson. You could have content for all three topics, but only discuss the content of the topic chosen by most of the class. These types of choices make students feel empowered and increase their motivation to active participation within the lesson. Poll questions can be used as a temperature check to see how students are feeling about their confidence when engaging a new skill, or their knowledge about a topic just discussed in the lesson. A Poll question is an excellent way to engage a student with your topic without requiring a right answer. Students will feel less stress when you incorporate these types of questions in your lesson and you can be sure to get 100% participation.

Collaborate Board

Every 21st Century virtual classroom must promote collaboration. The Collaborate Board makes it effortless to increase the possibilities for students to review and add to the perspectives of other students on an academic topic. Just post a question that gets the students thinking and wait patiently for their responses. The Collaborate Board even allows you to post images. For example, you can have a student complete a PhET simulation lab, they take a screenshot of their final product, and post their screenshot lab results. Students would go ahead to provide comments on each other's progress. They get to see images from the various approaches other students took and their brain expands with these multiple data points to deepen their understanding on the topic. It is also great for just checking with students about questions they may still have, how they feel about what they have learned, and steps they will take to deepen their understanding of the content. Again, this is a tool that focuses on the process of learning and promotes an atmosphere that supports multiple ways of thinking. It is a great tool for brainstorming and the results can easily be shared to other web-based mediums used for the course. You can also make the responses anonymous by hiding student names. This way, they can feel safe to share their opinions and perspectives.

Flipgrid

When an educator cannot see their students, this is a real barrier to seeing the student as an individual learner with unique needs and skills sets. Flipgrid gives students a voice and helps virtual educators to make connections more easily. Flipgrid is a tool used to allow discussions or reflection on academic topics through video. You must set up an account with Flipgrid first before you can use this feature in Nearpod. Some students are nervous about recording a video of themselves. Initially, you may want to allow them to record their voice only, until they build their confidence to create a video response. For starters, it is best to set the video to moderator view only, so that only the teacher can view the videos. This will decrease potential stress among some students. It also works when the number of students in a group is limited, to help build an online community within your class and to feel safe to share their opinions with their classmates.

To embed Flipgrid within a lesson, you must have both the group discussion URL and the official teacher URL, which will be in the browser of the teacher Flipgrid account. Once both URLs are copied over, you will just need your students to validate either a Gmail account or a Microsoft email account to gain access to Flipgrid. Discussion will never be the same in your virtual classroom once you start incorporating the power of students' voice in your digital lessons. Flipgrid offers many innovative ideas on ways to incorporate the tool in any academic course.

KEY POINT

We reviewed five content features and five activity features that you need to use as soon as possible. The top ten features are:

1. Interactive Video: Create meaningful discussions with videos that embed questions for natural pauses, to discuss what they have just reviewed.
2. Slides: Create content slides that differentiate your content by using text, image, video, and audio to enhance your content.
3. Web Content: Insert any website by copying and pasting the URL into the web content tool to offer a seamless experience for your students and incorporate more relevant media within your lessons.

4. Slideshow: Insert mini discussion slides that promote small group discussions and create opportunities for students to interact socially with content.

5. Virtual Reality Field Trips: Create more real-world connections to academic topics by emerging students into real life places or settings that make them think deeper about content presented.

6. Draw- It: Import any document or image and use it as a background image for students to draw, write, or type on the image to demonstrate mastery.

7. Open Ended Question: Create ways for students to evaluate and analyze content in a safe way that promotes active participation.

8. Polling Tool: Solicit feedback from students on a variety of topics and use it to give students choice on topics covered in live class sessions.

9. Collaborate Board: Promote multiple perspectives and showcase students' efforts with this tool.

10. Flipgrid: Gives students a voice in your virtual class, by allowing video discussions and reflections through the free tool Flipgrid.

In the next chapter, we will take time to reflect on key points we have covered and discuss an action plan for your next steps in transforming your virtual teaching with Nearpod.

CHAPTER TWELVE: REFLECTION

You never achieve success unless you like what you are doing. – **Dale Carnegie**

Do you feel empowered to start using Nearpod now? Fill in the sheet below with Next Steps, what I plan to try and just know the support is here for you to get started transforming your virtual classroom and becoming the fearless educator that I know you are inside.

REFLECTION QUESTIONS

Reflection Question?	Response
What is one thing you plan to apply immediately in your virtual classroom?	
What percentage of my students participate on a regular basis in my lesson? What	

percentage do I want my lesson participation to be?	
What are my strongest instructional practices? How will Nearpod help me enhance them?	
What are the top 3 features you will use in your lessons over the next 30 days?	
Why do you want to use Nearpod in your virtual classroom?	
What benefits do you feel Nearpod will help bring to your instructional practice?	

How will you use Nearpod to help differentiate your lessons?	
What are you committed to do with Nearpod over the next 60 days?	
Name one teacher or mentor that will help you stay accountable to your action steps.	

NEXT STEPS ACTION PLAN

I have created a basic checklist to help you get started in launching your first lesson in Nearpod. Be sure to check off the items as you complete them. This will gradually build your confidence in your new skills and help you track areas you may want to revisit or review more until you feel confident with that application of Nearpod. You do not need to follow the action steps in order, but it is there to serve as a guide in helping you take the theory of teaching with Nearpod—to putting these concepts into practical steps for you.

Action Step	Notes	Completed (✓) Date
Read Beginner's Guide to Nearpod		
Login into Nearpod		
Search Nearpod Library for suitable lessons to use in a lesson or for a Differentiated Lesson		
Customized a Ready-Made lesson in Nearpod		
Commit to practice creating lessons in Nearpod at least 15 minutes a day for 2 weeks		
Create a lesson in Google Slides		

Select Content Slides to add Audio to, for example, provide instructions or explain a concept		
Launch a Customized Ready-Made Lesson		
Review a lesson Report and reflect on what went well and what you want to change		
Find a ready-made lesson and create three differentiate learning options (Challenge, Practice, Reteach)		
Share a student report in a Teacher-Parent Conference or during a data chat with your grade level		

Watch a how-to video on a feature you want to practice more		
Give students a survey to give you feedback on your Nearpod lessons		
Seek to become a Nearpod Certified Educator after you have launched at least 5 lessons		
Add your own action step		

PURPOSE

The purpose of reflection is to help you think about where you are and where you want to be. Spend some time answering the reflection questions, so that you understand what your starting point is and can better measure your results after you start using this tool. Do not skip this part. This will help you harness the mental energy to do the physical work of applying the techniques you have learned in this book. You must find your motivation. The reflection questions are there to guide you in your conversation with yourself. Everything we do starts with a conversation. I hope the conversation you have motivates you to get started using this tool and not allow it to accumulate dust and just be another thing in your educational cabinet.

Once you have completed your reflection questions, you have a list of possible action steps that you can transfer into goals to help you build your confidence one step at a time. Just commit to getting started and map out at least three steps in your first 30 days trial. As you try those three steps, keep repeating them until you feel comfortable. A better approach would be to add another three steps to your action plan after you have mastered that step. Each day, it will become less stressful as you become more powerful in your stills as a virtual teacher, who finds joy in transforming the learning experiences of students.

KEY POINT

You need to reflect in order to apply and grow as a virtual educator. Always make time to reflect on your progress in mastering this power tool. Spend time mapping out a mental picture of what you have learned. Select action steps that fit your strengths and help you increase your efficiency as an educator. Those you fail to plan, plan to fail. I hope you will be the opposite and use this chapter as a tool to help you plan why and how you will use Nearpod to transform virtual teaching in your respected grade(s) and subject area(s).

Chapter Thirteen: Beyond Nearpod

Your aspirations are your possibilities. – **Samuel Johnson**

The year 2020 changed the way we do education. In those challenging times, parents and teachers were forced to make hard decisions about how students were educated and how best to do that to keep everyone safe. Although some districts went back to face-to-face instruction, many parents were fearful of outbreaks in school and wanted to take extra precautions to keep their child safe. Many choose virtual education for their child, while some parents were forced to choose virtual due to no other options. Many teachers may have been asked to return to the classroom, but they choose to resign due to not feeling safe—while other teachers were not given the option to return to their classrooms. All of these situations merit empathy. None of us wants to be forced to do something without having options or alternatives. Through all of this, teachers are still tasked with helping students to learn. Parents are still tasked with supporting teachers and ensuring learning is still taking place, without a teacher present. If they don't learn anything, we need to help students cope with these new social and emotional challenges, giving them hope that their learning will still serve them now and in the future.

Teachers have a new commission on their shoulders, to boldly go where no educator has gone before. We are pioneering new instructional strategies and having deeper conversations about the essentials of an education that enables students to use and apply what they learn in their classrooms and use that information to contribute to society in an ethical and practical way. As educators, we must focus on *why* we choose to be teachers and use that *why* in refueling the desire to learn new ways to deepen students' learning. We must use that *why* to collaborate more with our colleagues, especially in problem solving challenges, and use that why to help us navigate successfully during these turbulent times. Your *why* must go beyond receiving a paycheck, as this can easily be shaken and with no reason, you can never get to the *what* nor the *how.* Your *why* is what you must fall, back on when you feel unsure—when you feel like it is too much for you to handle. There are future adults who are depending on us to shape their present circumstances and paint a picture of hope and dignity.

This semester, you may not have all the resources you need to do your job the best way, however, you can turn your focus to what resources are available to enable you to still do an effective job. We often complain about what we do not have, but I highly recommend you focus on what you do have and count it as a resource to help you accomplish your *why.* Whether you are using an existing online curriculum to administer your lessons or creating your own standards-based lessons, you are still the most critical component in helping students feel confident about what they are learning and ensuring they are academically successful. Use your live and self-paced lesson as a tool to engage students in ways we can only imagine. Be the facilitator and guide of their learning and continue to challenge yourself to learn new instructional strategies, and to use educational tools that will help them make more meaningful connections to content and real-world applications. Let them experience the struggle of learning something challenging but rising to the occasion to feel accomplishment from the labor of utilizing the most intelligent tool we were given—our brain.

The work you do goes beyond Nearpod, yet Nearpod can serve as your power tool in building lasting foundations without compromising the process of rigorous thinking. We need more educators to step up their game and embrace power tools such as Nearpod, to increase student engagement and truly spark their learning for a lifetime.

CLOSING

It has been a pleasure to share with you my passion for Nearpod and how it transformed my virtual teaching experience. In the future, Nearpod will become an essential tool of every classroom, whether virtual or in a regular classroom setting. You have the knowledge and the power to impact students in a more innovative way. It is truly a simple tool that is here to help make the toughest job of teaching, a source of joy and pleasure. I look forward to hearing your stories soon, of how Nearpod has helped transform your virtual classroom.

Change is the law of life and those who look only to the past or present are certain to miss the future. – **John F. Kennedy**

CHAPTER FOURTEEN: FAQ

Learn from yesterday, live for today, hope for tomorrow. The important thing is not to stop questioning. – **Albert Einstein**

Here are some of the most frequently asked questions about getting started with Nearpod.

1. How do my students see my web conferencing tool and Nearpod at the same time?

A: Have each application open on your computer and click on the restore down tap in the top right corner, left to the X button. Once the restore down button is clicked, your students can resize their Nearpod screen. Follow the same process for the web conferencing screen. It may be helpful to provide the students with a video tutorial to reduce any confusion.

2. Will each student have a Nearpod account?

A: Only teachers have Nearpod accounts. You will not be able to message students or provide individual feedback in the program. It is critical that you either enable the auto-fill name feature in the lesson settings, or have your students enter their first and last names before joining the session.

3. Can I assign a co-teacher for one of my lessons?

A: Currently, Nearpod does not have a co-teacher option. You can share the lesson with a teacher by generating a presentation link from the share option under the three dots in the left corner of your lesson. Canvas features a co-teacher option that will allow you to view student responses in real time.

4. If I get the Free Silver account, is there a storage limit?

A: Yes, storage space is limited to 100 MB for a free account and 20MB per lesson. Your best option is to create your presentations in Google Slides and import the presentation to Nearpod where you can add the interactive features. When your account is approaching its limit, delete the old Nearpod lessons knowing you still have the presentation saved to your Google Drive.

5. Are there any other limitations with a free account?

A: You can only have a maximum of 40 participants per code. The Google Ad on feature is not available for free accounts either. From December 2020, Nearpod offers access to their pre-made lessons that you can develop in Self-Paced and Front-of-the-Class Mode. Having at least a Gold account is the most ideal situation in order to access more storage. This site offers update information on pricing and features per package (https://nearpod.com/pricing).

6. Will my students' work be saved if I do not finish the lesson?

A: All student work is automatically saved in the reports section even if you get disconnected from the lesson. If you do not have time to complete a part of the lesson, you can generate the same code for the lesson and start on the slide that you want. You will be able to generate another report for this lesson that will have the work the students completed that day.

7. Where should I start?

A: Start where you feel the most comfortable with creating content first to keep your nerves at bay. If you have already created content, simply import the PPT or Google Slides into Nearpod and add a few interactive features based on what you want the students to learn or do. You can also find a pre-existing icebreaker or warm-up lesson in Nearpod's library and launch that with your students.

8. Is there an easy way to share a code with my class if I do not use a Learning Management System?

A: Once you are in your web conferencing tool, you may share the link in the chat or post a slide with directions with the code. This is a new routine for your students, so I highly suggest you use an easy icebreaker activity to have them practice joining a lesson. It takes only a few tries before it becomes a regular classroom habit.

9. How do you grade a Nearpod lesson?

A: The best way to use Nearpod is as a formative assessment. Allow students to inform you of what they need in real time and have support ready to meet their needs. Students will be more willing to participate knowing that the information is being used to help them understand the content better. I try not to assign too many grades from Nearpod as many schools have built-in assessment tools with their textbook providers. I highly recommend providing participation points for students who complete all activities within the lesson. Occasionally I will create a graded assessment, but it will be a standalone Nearpod lesson and I provide students with advance notice about it.

10. How can students see their work?

A: Since students do not have accounts, they cannot access the PDF report of their work. If students want to refer to their work after a lesson, I recommend you enable the note taking feature where they can have their notes emailed or saved to a storage drive. They can also take a snapshot or screenshot of their work and paste it into a document for future reference.

11. What happens if my lesson code expires?

A: Self-Paced codes have a 1-year expiration date. You decide when they expire up to one year. If it is a live lesson, there is a 14-day expiration period. You can also generate another code and update any documents shared with the students.

12. What other LMS platforms does Nearpod integrate with?

A: Nearpod integrates seamlessly with Google Classroom, Clever SSO, Remind, Canvas, Schoology, Blackboard, Itslearning, and Microsoft Teams. Some of these platforms can only be used with a School or District level subscription.

13. Can I copy and paste content from two different already made Nearpod lessons?

A: No. Due to copyright, you cannot copy content from one already made Nearpod lesson to another. You can, however, add additional content slides to the lesson.

14. What is the best way to play an interactive video in Nearpod?

A: If you have a video with no discussion questions, I recommended the "Play on their device" option. Otherwise, I recommend the "Play on my device" option. This is the only way to ensure that every student will see the same content and get the questions at the same time.

15. Can I live annotate on a Nearpod slide?

A: No, Nearpod does not have a whiteboard option, however there are two alternatives. You can create a Jamboard and insert the link under the Web Content feature. You could then screen share or know that each student can see what anyone contributes to the Jamboard. You can also insert a Draw It with your preferred background. Converting your view to Student View will allow you to use Draw It as an annotation tool.

16. How can I see the questions in a Quiz after students complete it?

A: Click on the answer choice letter and the question will appear. You can also click share and each student will be able to review each question and see the correct and incorrect choices.

17. Does Nearpod offer a private chat feature to students?

A: No, since Nearpod is an interactive presentation tool, it does not have the functions of a web conferencing tool. Most web conferencing tools will already have private chat as a feature.

18. Where can I find the answers to video questions?

A: Video questions are available through a link in your report. It will not be in PDF format; it will direct you back to the video and you will need to click on each dot to see responses to the question. The goal of interactive videos is to help students recall prior knowledge and engage them with the content. I recommend teachers do not use this feature as a grading tool.

19. Can I edit a Google Slide directly in Nearpod?

A: You cannot make direct edits to content from Google Slides in Nearpod. You would need to edit slide content directly in Google Slides and, either import the slides as a PPT, or use the Add On feature.

20. Can I trim an existing YouTube video in Nearpod?

A: Yes, you can. When you insert the YouTube link, there will be an option to trim the video content.

21. When is the best time to use Time to Climb?

A: You can use it as a review for a module or chapter, as an icebreaker, or as a way to revise prior knowledge before starting a lesson.

22. How can I show the question in an interactive video?

A: The video will automatically pause where you have inserted a question. However, you must click on the dot for the question to display on the teacher screen.

23. What is the best way to present a Nearpod lesson virtually?

A: If all your students can connect to the lesson, I recommend not sharing your screen until you get to a Collaborate Board or an interactive video. Live Participation Mode is best for a live virtual class. Self-Paced is only recommended for the differentiated portion of your lesson or for homework after class.

24. Can I start a synchronous live participation lesson and then switch to a student paced lesson?

A: Yes, you can. You simply need to end your live participation lesson, and then generate a code for a self-paced lesson and share it with your students. The work from the live participation lesson will be saved in a separate report from the self-paced lesson. Be sure to turn off the "must respond to each activity" option in your lesson settings so students can start on the slide you left off in the live session lesson.

25: What can students do if they show as a disconnected student?

A: If a student shows up red in your participant list, have them refresh their screen by pressing the circled arrow in the top left corner of their browser window. If this does not work, have the student re-click the link to log back into the lesson.

26: Can I design a content lesson right in Nearpod?

A: Yes, you can. Use the Add a Slide feature and choose one of the 7 background themes available. You can insert videos, GIFs, images, or text directly onto the slide.

27: Can students respond to questions verbally?

A: Yes, they can. If you create an open-ended question, you can enable the student voice response option.

28: Can a timer be used in a self-paced lesson?

A: No. Currently, timers can only be used in Live Participation mode sessions.

29: What is the best way to provide a hyperlink document in Nearpod?

A: You can create a Google doc and insert your links there, and then create a shareable link from the document to insert in the Web Content feature. Or you create a Google

Slide and insert your hyperlinks there and create a shareable link but change the ending work in the link from edit to preview. Lastly, insert that new shareable link in the Web content feature.

30: What is the best way to grade an open-ended response?

A: The best way to grade an open-ended response is to download the CSV formatted report of the lesson. It will automatically create a grade column next to the open-ended response for you to insert a grade or score.

31: Where can I go for more support in creating engaging Nearpod lessons?

A: You can join the Nearpod Educators Facebook group and post questions there. You can also sign up for a more in-depth online course at oliviaodileke.com/nearpod where I will walk you through the fundamentals of this book and offer more feedback unique to your situation.

RESOURCES

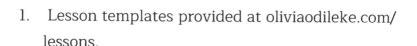

1. Lesson templates provided at oliviaodileke.com/ lessons.
2. To access more in-depth video tutorials of chapters 4-9 go to oliviaodileke.com/nearpod.
3. To receive a 3-month Gold subscription go to nearpod.com/redeem and enter the code NP-Olivia Odileke.
4. For a list of ready to watch Nearpod tutorials visit https://vimeo.com/nearpod/videos.
5. Visit oliviaodileke.com or inspire@oliviaodileke.com to contact me directly with your transformational classroom stories.

ACKNOWLEDGMENTS

Thanks to my husband Godwin for the late-night talks and the helpful feedback on my written chapters.

Thanks to my editor Jessica Raymond, who has helped my words have deeper meaning and impact due to your exceptional grammar skills. Keep doing you, girl. She can be reached at jessicaraymond233@gmail.com.

Thanks to Jakiera, for helping me fine tune my book title and believing in my ability to inspire more virtual teachers to succeed.

Thanks to my publisher for making the publishing of this book easy and stress free.

Thanks to Kevin Snyder and Kent Julian, for inspiring me to write a book that serves the needs of teachers and helps me make my contribution to the field of education.

Thanks to the founders of Nearpod, for never giving up on their idea and helping teachers do the toughest job in the world.

ABOUT THE AUTHOR

———— ♦◇♦ ————

Olivia Odileke's sole mission is to transform virtual learning experiences for teachers one at a time. She is a native of Belle Glade, Florida. Her educational background consists of a B.S in Industrial Engineering from the University of Central Florida in Orlando, and a M.Ed. in Instructional Technology from Florida Atlantic University in Boca Raton, Florida. She holds a vast array of professional experience, dedicated to the educational sector and has spent over a decade working as an educator in Title I Schools in Florida. For the past few years, she has dedicated her expertise to work as a virtual teacher trainer, with K-12 Schools. Olivia Odileke is also the owner of Kampus Insights (kampusinsights.com), a company created to provide teachers with additional support and training to help bridge the gap created by the modernization of technology.

Olivia Odileke loves making Ed Tech and virtual teaching easier for teachers. She serves as a national Teacher Trainer for the online school Stride Inc. She has personally trained over 3,000 teachers and continues to seek ways to innovate education. She is a Certified Level 3 Trainer for Nearpod, Google Certified Educator, and has served as an HMH Regional Math Consultant. She serves as the Google Educators Groups Leader for Florida. She has written over 30 published lessons for Cpalms.org, Nearpod, and Pearson. She holds a M.Ed. in Instructional Technology. All her experience has led her to becoming an expert in virtual education and the tech tools educators can use to drive student learning and curiosity.

Olivia Odileke is available for speaking engagements with her featured Keynote *Becoming a Fearless Educator in a Virtual Learning Environment* and other topics that can be customized to meet the needs of your educator audience.

Made in the USA
Las Vegas, NV
28 February 2021